LET PRAYER

change

YOUR LIFE

LET PRAYER *change* YOUR LIFE

BECKY TIRABASSI

OLIVER
NELSON

THOMAS NELSON PUBLISHERS
Nashville · Atlanta · London · Vancouver

Published in Nashville, Tennessee, by Thomas Nelson, Inc., Publishers, and distributed in Canada by Word Communications, Ltd., Richmond, British Columbia. Originally titled *Releasing God's Power*.

Quotation from Arthur T. Pierson, *George Muller of Bristol*, Fleming H. Revell Company, used by permission.

Quotation from *I Will Lift Up Mine Eyes*, © 1937 Glenn Clark, Harper & Row, Publishers, Inc., used by permission.

Scripture quotations are taken from the HOLY BIBLE, NEW INTERNATIONAL VERSION®. Copyright © 1973, 1978, 1984 by International Bible Society. Used by permission of Zondervan Publishing House. All rights reserved.

Scripture quotations marked NKJV are taken from THE NEW KING JAMES VERSION. Copyright © 1979, 1980, 1982, 1990, Thomas Nelson, Inc., Publishers.

Verses marked TLB are taken from *The Living Bible*, copyright 1971 by Tyndale House Publishers, Wheaton, IL. Used by permission.

Library of Congress Cataloging-in-Publication Data

Tirabassi, Becky, 1954–
    Let prayer change your life : how you can release God's power/
Becky Tirabassi.
        p.   cm.
    Rev. ed. of: Releasing God's power. c1990.
    ISBN 0-7852-7721-8 (pbk.)
    1. Prayer—Christianity.   I. Tirabassi, Becky, 1954–   Releasing
God's power.   II. Title.
BV220.T57   1992
248.3'2—dc20   91-44834
                                                                CIP

Printed in the United States of America.

15 16 17 18 19 20 — 00 99 98 97 96 95

Contents

A DEEPER WALK

Acknowledgment

To

Roger, my mentor and best friend.

Thank you for investing
in my life and ministry
for the past seventeen years!

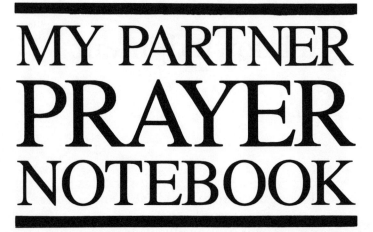
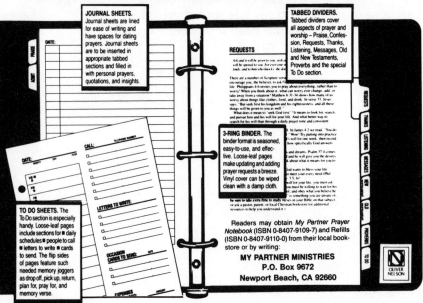

Introduction

n convinced that the practice of prayer in a
's life is an incredible, virtually untapped
ource. Not only am I convinced because of my
l experiences, but the lives of many who have
mmitted to the discipline of daily prayer, dur-
before our present day, validate that I am not
1 my discovery!

e following pages of this book, I pray, will serve
iration and motivation to each reader to con-
ie power of prayer through a daily appointment
od as an essential and integral part of every
tories, sermon excerpts, prayers, and quotes
ien of the faith such as Peter Marshall, George
r, Andrew Murray, and many others will be a
constant source of encouragement and exhortation for
us to hold onto when our resistance gets low and our
endurance in prayer wavers.

Upon recognition that prayerlessness was sin in
my life, I was deeply touched by God to make a commitment to pray for one hour a day. Eleven years (and
many "hours") later, God has changed my personality
and character, increased my faith through unbelievable answers to prayer, called me to accountability in

innumerable areas, and given me a vivid vision of possibilities for His will in my life. Having been a teenage alcoholic, I know that this disciplined prayer life is a work of the Holy Spirit within me, not a privileged performance that I have perfected.

The unfolding of the discipline of prayer in my life was an unexpected surprise. I'm not the kind of person you would normally find sitting still for one hour, much less praying all that time. But because of prayer, the last eleven years have been an incredible journey with Christ. To help you clearly understand prayer and its power from my perspective—that of a Christian woman, not a scholar, not a pastor, not a seminary student—I believe God has given me five parts in which to explain prayer.

The first part concerns the discovery of prayer. This part discusses what it is and what it isn't. How do you view prayer? Do you see prayer as a believer's power source or a source of boredom? From the beginning of this book, be challenged to change!

Eleven years ago I was at a convention workshop where many speakers were talking about prayer. Had I known the convention would even be threaded with the word prayer, I probably wouldn't have gone. Prayer was never a big interest to me as a Christian, yet when someone said, "Prayerlessness is sin in a believer's life," I had to take that statement to heart. I had to say, "Either I believe this as truth, or I don't believe it."

What do you believe about prayer? Where do you stand on this topic?

The second part focuses on what happens from decision to discipline. Another characteristic of my life was not being disciplined. *Discipline* is a serious word much like *prayer*. It means work. It means count a cost. Those are things my particular personality avoids if at all possible.

Yet, when confronted with the fact that I did believe that prayerlessness was sin, I was forced to make a

10

decision. If Jesus Christ was the priority that I said He was in my life to other people, to my friends, and to my family, why in the world did I spend so little time with Him on a daily basis?

You make time for those you love. You make time for what you consider a priority. Think over your last day . . . your last week . . . your last month. What did you make time for? It may be different from what you say your priorities are, but what you actually did tells you what you really feel strongly about. I had to stand back and say, "Then where is my time with God in all of this?"

At that juncture I made the decision to pray for an hour a day for the rest of my life. That may sound pious. That may sound spiritual. It was neither. I felt a great need to know God and love God like I had when I first met Him. I was exuberant when I met Christ. I was changed! I was excited! I was renewed! I dropped unsavory habits left and right. Why as an older Christian did I consider spending time with God a discipline?

My decision to pray an hour a day took me knee deep into discipline. How do you get a sanguine, Type A young woman to sit down for one hour and pray?

There were immediate differences within my life that kept me going. My priorities changed. I couldn't help but meet with God every day and let Him filter through my "to do" list, which at the time included a few hours of watching soap operas and at least an hour of chatting on the phone. I could probably add twenty minutes if I added up all the time that I stood in front of the refrigerator wondering what was in there! My time became very important to me because, all of a sudden, I felt it was important to God.

Psalm 90:12 says, "Teach us to number our days aright, that we may gain a heart of wisdom." It didn't take long—probably a week before I realized, "Oh, my goodness, you're wasting a lot of time for the kingdom of God."

11

My perspective on God changed.
He was no longer too small.
  Too strict.
    Or too far away.
     He is near.
      He is here.
       He is always with me.
       He is powerful.
        He is the Creator of the world.
        He is the Creator of me.

Somehow in my fast-paced, busy little Christian life I rarely stopped and said, "You are God. Show me the way to go. You've already planned it. I want to know." No, I hustled and bustled through every day and then figured out at the end of the day (after I had "crashed and burned" a few times) that I would have been better off to consult Him earlier in the day.

Not that I didn't know God. Not that I wouldn't have told you, "I love Him." But I was truly falling in love with Him as a person, not as a wizard of Oz machine that pumps smoke and firmly says, "No!"

My personality changed. How can you spend time with someone and not be influenced by that person's character? I spend one week with teenagers, and I walk away saying, "Like man, you're a cool dude. Totally, I mean . . ." I can hardly *not* talk like them. And they spend time with me, and they say (instead of slang words), "Oh, my goodness . . ."

How can you spend time with the person of God and not experience a change in your character and your personality? It is inevitable. What happened to me? A million swept-under-the-rug personality flaws flew out from everywhere, things I had been holding inside so that no one would see what I was really like.

Yes, I was the child of an alcoholic. Yes, I was an alcoholic myself. Those two things alone create enough for psychologists to spend years with someone. And yet, an hour a day with God began to unravel, unfold, reveal, and heal the mess that was within me in a gentle, positive, renewing way.

And my possibilities changed. I was no longer destined to live in a two-mile radius. Hopes and dreams, ideas and goals, plans and problems—all bombarded me so much that I had to do *something* about them. God was giving me ideas to change the world, my home, my church, and myself.

The person He has created you to be can be unleashed if you'll just spend time with Him. Perhaps it's time to go to the school of prayer, to get your education for where He wants to take you, by clinging to God on a daily basis, hearing His will, letting Him change your character and give you a plan (rather than your devising what feels right or sounds good to you). Prayer will illuminate the difference between knowing God's will and guessing about it.

The third part of this book is the design for prayer. We'll explore talking to God and recognizing His voice —one Christian's secret to a happy hour!

Hannah Whitall Smith wrote *The Christian's Secret of a Happy Life*. She was a woman who read the Bible and believed it. She tried it, tested it, and found it to be true. So it is with an hour in prayer. I have tried it, I have tested it, and I have found it to be the most significant life-changing experience I have had outside of my conversion to Christ. And that experience happens every single day.

From my commitment to pray an hour a day, God gave me a tool called *My Partner Prayer Notebook*. With that tool I became organized and accountable in my prayer life. I think it's one reason I've not missed a day in eleven years. It faces me every day. It reminds me. It encourages me. It calls out to me, "Come on . . ."

The fourth part is an adventure into the delights, desires, and dreams of your heart because of prayer.

13

We'll look at six powerful prayer principles as literal, scriptural promises in our walk and our relationship with God:

- Receiving prayer
- Believing prayer
- Revealing prayer
- Interceding prayer
- Agreeing prayer
- Persevering prayer

Those principles have led to mounds of miracles and open doors and onward dreams, not for me alone but for others who have practiced prayer. And they'll work for you, too!

The last section illustrates how to take a deeper walk with God. After eleven years of praying an hour a day, what has resulted for me?

I have a much deeper faith.

I've put my hope in the Word, literally.

I've learned to wait on God.

I've received daily direction.

And I've learned to feel love for God.

I urge you to release God's power through a new (or renewed) practice of prayer in your life. If, in fact, you are content with your fellowship with the Lord on a daily, perhaps hourly, basis, I trust this time will be refreshing. But if you open this book out of a deep hunger for effective, powerful prayer as the Bible details, be open to God's Holy Spirit and believe your life will never be the same because prayer does, prayer can, and prayer will change your life.

PART I

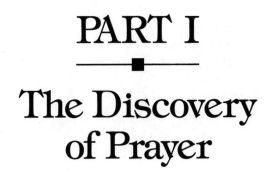

The Discovery
of Prayer

What It Is,
What It Isn't

Prayer—My Heartthrob?

I've been so dramatically changed and influenced by the discovery of prayer in my life that I've grown to agree with O Hallesby's conviction that "prayer is the heartthrob of a believer's life." Therefore, when the topic of prayer popped up in a casual dinner conversation with a younger Christian, I automatically asked my favorite mentorlike question, "How's your quiet time?" Her coy reply was, "Well, I'm not praying as much as I should or I ought . . ."

Though her response didn't seem out of the ordinary, it allowed me to identify the problem of *why* she was struggling with prayer. Her perspective on prayer, as mine had once been, was confused. Prayer had become something she felt she *had* to do rather than something she wanted, desired, needed, or longed to do.

The "Problem of Prayer"

Prayer is a word that probably creates a different picture in each person's mind. It seems briefly discussed and little practiced at many Christian gatherings, and often when it is presented, attendance is sparse or the event is heralded mostly by women, rarely by youths and men.

Why? Why, in this time of great need for revival, especially in the United States, does a power source for transformation and change—namely, prayer—get so little attention?

To answer that question, I needed to look only as far as myself. The reasons that prayer is pushed aside are varied and often based on misconceptions.

Misconception 1: "It's Boring!"

Prayer *on the surface* may seem boring. Perhaps it's the pure exhaustion of regular prayer that causes one to quit early without ever seeing the rewarding results of persevering prayer, or the boredom that prevails when group prayer sinks to monotone levels. And certainly falling asleep during prayer has been the experience of many a tired believer who reverently closes his eyes and winds up disrupting a prayer meeting or group due to loud snoring or snorting!

Oh, the mention of *prayer* quickly triggers "I've got to get out of here before I'm stuck" reactions in many people—perhaps because most of us are inspired and motivated by the excitement of evangelism, moving preaching, heart-throbbing music and testimony, and yet we possess little or no knowledge of the power released when one prays.

And wouldn't that just suit the enemy's cause? Disguise prayer as tedious, powerless, geriatric, and "religious," and you'll keep believers away from it ninety out of one hundred times.

But if prayer was so boring, why didn't the disciples ask Jesus how to perform miracles and healings—instead of asking Him how to pray (Luke 11)? If prayer was so boring and such a potential time-waster, why did Jesus Himself choose so often to spend time alone in prayer? Who started the rumor that prayer was boring, anyway?

Misconception 2: "Prayer Is Only for the Pious and the Spiritual."

Perhaps it's the thought that *I'm not good enough. God wouldn't talk to me! He certainly is busy enough without having to make time for me. Why I'm just . . ."* That misconception holds some truth, but we hold the key that unlocks that shut door.

Yes, it is a biblical statement that God does not listen if we cherish—or hold onto—sin in our hearts (Ps. 66:18), but the Word also states that confession of sin brings His forgiveness (1 John 1:9) and opens the gates of communication with our heavenly Father. Therefore, an incorrect attitude of humility suggests we can never be good enough for God to hear—or care for—us; but a broken, contrite, and *humble* heart is the way to the foot of the King's throne—and to our loving Father!

Misconception 3: "God Doesn't Always Answer Prayer."

Is God unable to meet our needs, reverse our circumstances, or change what appears to be impossible? At this point, it becomes a matter of one's perception of God or, better stated, *one's faith or belief in who God is.*

A lack of faith—in *anyone*—certainly decreases one's ability to trust in that person, and it appears to be no different with God. Those who believe God can't or won't answer prayer seem not to believe in the God of the Old and New Testaments. The Bible speaks boldly of a God

19

who performs miracles,
  brings the dead back to life,
    turns the sea into dry land,
      converts sinners to Christ, and
        assigns them as evangelists and
          apostles!
The God spoken of by the prophets and priests of the Old Testament is all-powerful, all-knowing, and always present, and the God of the New Testament manifested in the person of Jesus Christ is personal *and* powerful, able to forgive the darkest sins and to heal the deadliest diseases. It then becomes one's personal faith to believe that prayer to God as validated in Scripture not only will be heard, but will be answered! In other words, God *can*, God *will*, and God *does* do the impossible when we pray. Do you believe that?

Misconception 4: "My Prayer Has No Power."

But in truth, the vast majority of us fall into the classification of ignorance—not rebellion, not conscious avoidance, but simply not knowing the truth about the power released when one prays. Ignorance about prayer automatically sets a good deal of believers into the powerless category of Christian living called "prayerlessness." Who would have imagined that not praying could be considered sin in a believer's life?

Certainly we all enter into a personal relationship with Christ through various individual circumstances: through childhood religion classes, by parental spiritual nurturing, as a youth in catechism or on retreat, through an altar call, by method of mass evangelism or renewal, just to list a few possibilities. Yet how many of us were presented with the spiritual discipline of prayer as an incredible, powerful, exciting, life-changing, and life-directing daily experience with and expression to the living God? I think it's safe to assume only a fortunate few were taught and trained to pray by a godly mentor, parent, pastor, or teacher who had experienced prayer in that very way, *or there would be many more of us who love to pray!*

The current result: Powerless Christians who find Bible reading *and* praying too time-consuming for their daily lives, who think those things are okay on Sundays or when an urgent need arises or when all else has failed.

Results of Prayerlessness

Just as the Public Safety Department of the Automobile Club of Southern California has developed a survey indicating possible problem drinkers—answer one yes and consider it a warning to your problem, two yes answers and you just might be, and three yes answers mean you most likely are a problem drinker—so O. Hallesby has developed a list of the dangerous results of prayerlessness:

- We have more "world" in our thoughts.
- We feel farther away from God.
- We have less "God" talk in our conversations with others.
- Slowly an unwilling or rebellious spirit creeps into our personality.
- Sin doesn't sting as much, because it is less honestly confessed.
- We deal with sin as the world does, by hiding it!

Isn't it *almost* humorous how those with the disease are the least likely to pick up a book or be involved in a setting where they would ever hear a convicting message? But like some reading this book even now, if I had read a list of the results of neglected prayer, such as the one above, perhaps I would have been caught long before I had reached a serious, spiritual drought.

It's too bad that the word *prayer* on the cover of a book or in the title of a workshop can keep us from what has the potential to radically release a supernatural power to change our lives while here on earth. So what is left? Not much! But that's where it seems that the victory over prayerlessness begins . . . with helplessness.

Andrew Murray in his classic, *The Prayer Life*, devotes numerous chapters to the issue of prayerlessness in a believer's life. A sincere study of his findings, consolations, rebukings, and encouragement offers great hope to someone discouraged by self-effort and continuous lack of victory in the pursuit of a *true* prayer life.

He says,

> My advice to you is: Give over your restlessness and effort; *fall helpless* at the feet of the Lord Jesus; He will speak the word, and your soul will "live." If you have done this, then, second, comes the message: "This is but the beginning of everything. *It will require deep earnestness,* and the exercise of all your power, and a *watchfulness* of the entire heart—eager to detect the least backsliding. Above all, it will require a *surrender* to a life of self-sacrifice that God really desires to see in us and which He will work out for us."

Bottom line, he powerfully suggests,

> If we recognize, in the first place, that a right relationship to the Lord Jesus, above all else, *includes prayer,* with both the desire and power to pray according to God's will, then we have something which gives us the right to rejoice in Him and to rest in Him (emphasis added).

Once again, like alcoholics faced with the truth of the problem, we as believers are forced to examine our own prayer lives in the privacy of our hearts. It is only then, with complete dependency upon the Holy Spirit and *His* renewing, revealing power, that we can allow God to speak to us, perhaps as we have never before experienced Him, regarding our relationship with Him and our prayer lives.

Perhaps it is time for you to

- Let God convince you that prayerlessness in a believer's life is sin.
- Admit your helplessness.
- Confess your sin and accept God's forgiveness.
- Be encouraged that you are not alone in the world, but you may be a trailblazer for prayer in your home, youth group, church, organization, city, synod, or state.

Then as C. S. Lewis put it, be challenged to change with "a fellow-patient in the same hospital who, having been admitted a little earlier, could give some advice."

Challenged to Change

The best place to start is just to tell you how it happened in my life. God's power was released following my decision to pray for one hour a day for the rest of my life. That was eleven years ago. So 4,015 hours with the Lord later I have great things to report to you.

It was my seventh year as a Christian. Even reflecting on the thought of coming to know Christ always elicits a deep emotional reaction within my soul. Having been converted to Christ as a teenage alcoholic in a dramatic way and subsequently catapulted into youth ministry, I never really knew any other way to live as a Christian other than in a *daily* relationship, always expecting Him at every turn.

A Fading Faith . . .

But somehow, somewhere, that zeal and fervor I once couldn't hide if I tried had faded into fond memories without my awareness. It wasn't until February of 1984 that I recognized a real change in myself—both outwardly and inwardly.

A list of my character flaws would take the better part of this page, but they weren't all of the problem. I was struggling with relationships, weight control, and thought life. Even the prospects for my future seemed like grains of sand strewn and scattered about randomly rather than a pathway warmly lighted and especially cut from stone expressly for me to follow.

Integrity, focus, humor, and joy in serving the Lord had almost disappeared, causing me to fit right in with the world.

A Glimpse that Produced Only a Grimace

The "baby Christian" pace of excitement, miracles, and the daily discovery of God no longer was the rule; it was now the exception.

Somewhere along the way I had fallen prey to the enemy's voice that said, "Mature Christians don't believe that God does miraculous things in a believer's life for *all* of life." I was beginning to adopt part of "the honeymoon was over" philosophy.

My once-crucified inherent weaknesses—jealousies, comparisons, workaholism, and anger—were resurfacing. Nagging at me, like hunger pains, the least bit of self-evaluation or personal spiritual inventory brought two things to the surface: (1) *what used to be* and (2) *what was no more!*

Upon my conversion to Christ in 1976, my initial need for God was so great that I considered Him my constant companion and friend—almost visualizing His presence with me at all times. In the beginning of our relationship, I would consult Him on the most extraordinary and seemingly impossible opportunities and blindly trust His power to intervene. For instance, in my first month as a believer, I believed He wanted me to return to my parents' home—to show them my new life in Christ—so I simply asked Him for a way from California to Ohio. Daily I prayed that He would help me to get home.

A used car salesman had always been friendly

toward me, though we had little in common other than our business relationship. After I told him of my conversion to Christ, he looked at me as if I wasn't "all there," perhaps thinking drugs had altered my emotional and mental state. Whereas once I had been a party-going, worldly young woman, now all I did was talk about my newfound Friend, Jesus.

When I told him that I felt God wanted me to return to Ohio, he only chuckled. My faith was very child-like at that point in time; therefore, I wasn't embarrassed because I felt God was as real as this man was, and if someone was going to laugh at me, I would prefer it be the used car salesman instead of God. Ironically, within the next few days, this salesman returned to my desk and said to me, "You won't believe this, but I have a friend in Ohio who owns a twenty-nine-foot motor home that has been in storage up in Oakland. He has been unable to transport it back to Ohio, and he wondered if you would be interested in driving it home to his car dealership in Ohio."

Well, I looked at my salesman friend and said, "Would I!" Immediately, I imagined my bike, furniture, silverware, clothes—everything—loaded into this motor home, saving shipping charges. A day or two later I received a telegram that authorized me to drive this motor home, free of charge, free of fuel charges, in order to get it back across the country. Though it could have seemed coincidental to some, in my new, young faith in Christ, I felt that my Friend, Jesus, had literally provided a way home for me—knowing that I didn't have any money to do it on my own.

With the same confident assurance that Jesus would show me His will in big decisions, I would inquire of my close Friend about the most minute and seemingly unimportant-to-anyone-else requests, such as what to wear, where to spend my free time, what I should talk to non-Christians about, and which sections I should read in the Bible. My basic question be-

26

came, "What would *You* have me do today, Lord?" You see, I had lived in the world so long and made so many decisions based on feelings, or on what others did and thought, that I became quickly dependent upon God's nudge of direction for every little detail of my life.

And with the same fervency, I was consumed with the Bible, understanding that if I wanted to hear God's voice, I *needed* to read His Word. I read incessantly, diligently searching for His advice on issues such as purity, honesty, and discipline—all areas that had troubled my "old" nature. Enthralled with the eye-opening stories of the early disciples in the book of Acts and the principles for daily Christian living as set forth by Jesus, Paul, and John, I took God's Word as literal and powerful, and I carried it with me everywhere.

From Burned Out to Turned Around!

Years later, as a youth worker, I mundanely pulled manuals off a shelf, referred to proven ministry methods rather than developed my own, read a bit of my Bible each night in bed (though it would often fall on my face, only to rudely wake me up), prayed occasionally for "a touch from God," and regularly fell asleep during prayer time with my husband.

How in the world did I get from one extreme to the other? I loved Jesus! I loved to talk about Him! I gladly evangelized! Except, except . . . even that had been conveniently shrugged off over the past few months. The burning flame of fire that at one time appeared to glow from within me was all but extinguished.

Oh, it wasn't that I didn't appear spiritual or think of myself as a "good" Christian. Each week I was regularly running two Bible studies and one youth group meeting. I attended church. I was the very active wife of the executive director of Youth For Christ, the mother of one, and the cheerleading coach at the local high school. That only proved a point. Not all the *things* done for God make one godly. So what was missing?

It was just as the first flicker of inner revival was igniting that my husband (and boss of seven years) and I were scheduled to attend a national Youth For Christ convention.

From Flicker to Flame

I always enjoyed a convention. Speakers, singing, challenge. Hmmm. Yes, if there ever was a time in my life when I needed a lift or renewal, it was then! Before leaving Cleveland for the convention in Chicago, I had come to the conclusion that this spiritual drought was the result of burnout—overwork, little rest, and too much responsibility. Therefore, I had purposed in my mind to quit the ministry. It seemed an appropriate time to leave the working world, relax, omit outside stress, and just be happy *inside*.

But the first speaker at the convention shocked me with his comment: "If you think it's time to quit, it's too soon!" This had happened to me before. Through a person, God was speaking to me. As if I were the only person in the room, the words from that one sentence resounded and echoed in my ears until I acknowledged that they were directly from God—to me.

God seemed to be saying, "Don't get up. Don't go anywhere. Don't daydream or pretend you don't hear My voice. You've been looking for answers, and I'm going to give them to you . . . though not what you might expect."

Sandwiched between perfect strangers, I didn't dare move. Without a friend to verbalize this experience to, I sat back, exhaled, then took the slow, deep breath of a person curious with anticipation. Though somewhat afraid of what God might say or do, I nervously awaited something unusual or supernatural to occur.

Prayer Attitude: Just not a Priority

Then it unfolded, on cue, but without rehearsal. Each keynote speaker had been asked to speak on how God had been at work in the Youth For Christ (YFC) organization over the previous forty years. Though none of them were given a more specific theme, there was one unexpected thread—especially for my ears— prayer.

Prayer? If the convention had been promoted as a *prayer* conference, I would have never considered attending it. Not that I didn't believe in prayer and its value for the Christian. I just had not, up to that point in time, considered prayer instrumental in my daily walk with Christ. Oh, I "prayed." I kept a journal of written conversations with the Lord, when in distress or trouble I regularly released an "I need HELP" prayer and often found myself asking God for a parking space close to a store entrance during a rain- or snowstorm, but sadly that was the extent of prayer in my Christian life.

Certainly, young, busy Christians shouldn't be expected to carry on with such a serious (and boring) discipline, should they? Prayer, to be perfectly honest, was not a priority—though it was a principle I believed in and encouraged others to do the same.

Prayer Action: Make it a Priority!

Like a bombshell, it hit with the second speaker.

Even as he began to share, his sincerity about God, ministry, and prayer became evident. He told of regular, daily intercession for the salvation of his neighbors. I was struck with the thought of his incredibly busy schedule and amazed that he *made time* to pray for his neighbors. I didn't even know my neighbor's names!

As he continued, his tone of voice rose and his intensity flared as he pounded out the words of James

4:2. Looking at those of us who needed to call on God's power most and probably used it least, he cried, "You do not have because you do not ask! James 4:2." I actually opened my Bible to the verse thinking that it couldn't really say that—at least, not in that way. It wasn't that blatant, was it? Then he choked up with tears and proceeded to impress upon the listeners the fervency of his message: "Prayerlessness, for the believer, is sin."

How he phrased it, said it, or convinced me, I'm still unsure, but the Holy Spirit began His own conviction upon my heart—and never stopped—until the last optional workshop of the convention on Saturday morning. I cried in silent shame and humiliation through every general session because of my lack of prayer, as each godly speaker related tremendous miracles of healing, incredible circumstances of God's intervention (for example, opening the doors of India to the gospel and YFC after a twenty-four-hour prayer vigil), and even the harvest of souls saved years later *due to daily, consistent prayers.*

Their stories magnified and illuminated the self-sufficient approach to ministry and daily Christian life that I was living because of the sin of prayerlessness. By then, only one word aptly described my state: *ashamed.* I was ashamed of myself for the audacity to lead Bible studies, evangelize, work for God daily, but spend *no* personal time with Him in prayer, in conversation, or even in confession.

Prayer Application: Not a Choice? Not an Option? A Must!

As the weekend came to a close, we were invited to choose from a list of various optional seminars. Like a neon light flashing on the pamphlet was a workshop on prayer. That would be my choice.

As my good friend and I were standing at the entrance to this workshop, laughter seemed appropriate to break up the serious mood of my desire to want to go into a workshop on prayer. Both of us had the feeling that the discipline of prayer was an extremely serious matter, but neither of us did anything that was that serious (at least up to that point in time).

Parting ways, I slowly entered the workshop feeling awkward and hesitant. I picked a seat in the back of the auditorium with the thought that I could still leave the room if it got too serious or boring.

Once again, tears flowed down my cheeks uncontrollably throughout the hour presentation on prayer as the speaker talked of the power available to a believer who prays. To make matters worse, no one else in the room seemed to react to the speaker with similar emotion, and my blubbering appeared out of place. I just couldn't pinpoint the root of all of this!

But God's work was being completed within me. Through the weekend and culminating with this workshop, I was indeed convinced that prayerlessness in the life of *this* believer was sin. If I truly believed that spending time with God in prayer was actually engaging in conversation with my Creator, Friend, Savior, Leader, and King, *why* would I overlook, avoid, forget, or fall asleep in the middle of prayers? If I truly wanted to be used by God to evangelize and disciple the world for Christ, why would I place so little emphasis on time alone with Him?

My perspective on prayer was changing.

I sat frozen as all three hundred workshop attendees filed out of the room. I was probably an interesting sight with streaked makeup and red puffy cheeks. I just didn't want to leave the room without making dramatic changes in my life, but where to start and how to maintain them seemed beyond my grasp.

Then a woman touched my shoulder, offering to pray with me, about . . .

I bowed my head, determined to make a lifelong

decision to . . . to . . . to . . . change, I guess. Change what? Change how?

Then words of prayer flowed from my mouth with the same intensity and mystery as my initial prayer for salvation had come so desperately from within me seven years earlier. Without premeditation, I made a decision in front of God and another person to pray for an hour a day for the rest of my life!

I knew myself too well. If I had given God a trial period to see if "I liked it" or if "it fit into my busy life," I would have allowed the decision to pray an hour a day to fizzle into a sweet memory as a "too difficult for me" discipline.

No, I sensed God's presence and provision in this decision, *and* I had been weighing the benefits of prayer in a believer's life versus life without it *all week long!* It was a hands-down decision to pursue the discipline.

Mentally drifting back to the seminar, I remembered a number of verses and principles about prayer the speaker had explained. Not a single verse had been new—Matthew 6:31–34; 7:7–8; and Philippians 4:6–7, 19—yet for the first time, those words were alive and fresh and inviting. Their practicality pierced me as I mentally walked with them through a typical day. As I toyed with actually believing them, they stunned me with their power.

An hour a day. I had to take a radical step closer to God. I took the plunge and left that room bathed afresh in the power of the Holy Spirit. It was all I could do to find Kinney, my friend, go to lunch, and pour out to her all that I felt God was saying to me. Something was coming alive within me. The relationship with God I had experienced as a young "on fire," baby Christian was aglow. That dependency, that willingness to be guided by God, to listen to Him, to share every thought with Him, was reignited within me as acceptable, not as childish. With the true style of an evangelist, I elaborated on all that I had heard and all I was certain that

God was going to do in my life because of prayer. We laughed, we cried, and both of us thought how special this convention had been—certain God had touched our lives.

It was to be beyond my wildest expectations what power God would release into my life from that day forward because of prayer, but first the discipline had to be mastered.

PART II

■

From Decision
to Discipline

CHAPTER

3

Knee Deep in Discipline

That first morning at home after the convention, without inspirational speakers, great music, or people's faces reminding me of my decision to pray, I walked into my kitchen after sending my son and husband off for the day. A little baffled, I thought: *Well, here I go, my first hour, but where do I start?*

Inexperienced in the classical spiritual disciplines, but not in the gift of gab, I chose to write my prayers. Writing kept me focused, allowing concentration while in conversation with the Lord—much like eye contact intensifies verbal communication—saving me from casual daydreaming and the inevitable distractions of household chores.

Before I sat down, I collected paper and pen and made a fresh pot of coffee. At that very moment, as if God knew exactly what I was about to do, on the radio echoed the regular jingle of the weekly program, "Chapel of the Air." Speaking was Karen Mains, the same woman who two days earlier and five hundred miles away had led the optional workshop on prayer that was *just beginning* to rearrange my daily life. To me, it was *no* coincidence. It was God, in His special and loving way, adding credibility to my decision. He had heard my convention prayer! Now He would be waiting for me.

I turned off the radio, took the phone off the hook, set the alarm on the stove to ring in one hour, and had my first "appointment" with God. Afraid I'd run out of things to say before my hour was up, I talked to God about all I could think of (my husband, our ministry, our Campus Life kids, our finances, our friends), then opened my Bible to read His words and hear His response. He spoke, and as I listened to His gentle, yet firm voice in Scripture, I recorded in writing what He said to me. I sensed that this was a long overdue appointment, and I was so grateful to be there. When the stove alarm buzzed, I was astonished at how quickly the time has passed and how my spirit was completely refreshed and satisfied.

Immediate Results

That afternoon I proceeded to exercise alone . . . something I had always planned to do on a regular basis but had never been disciplined to follow through with. Hmmm. An immediate result to a request in prayer, or just chance?

No, *chance* was no longer in my vocabulary. Time with God was *meant* to change my life, to bring
    resolve and
      results and
        renewal.
Why wouldn't I experience an immediate change?

I had just asked God to change my desires, even my appetite, to cause me to be disciplined in thought and in body, and I had been encouraged by the Word to pray about everything (Phil. 4:6), to trust God for a "transformed" mind (Rom. 12:2), and to walk blamelessly (Ps. 15) all through the day. Yes, He was speaking to me.

Ah, but that posed a new dilemma. Now the concept of *time* had much more significance in my daily life. For me to number my days aright (Ps. 90:12) meant that God was interested in my whole day—where I went, what I watched on TV or listened to on the radio, even how long I spent chatting on the phone.

I began to take a good look at my habits, choices, opportunities, interruptions, and commitments with a new, much more discerning mind. It seemed that every day mattered to God. And David in Psalm 139 seemed to validate that principle by stating God had preplanned our days even before our birth. Certainly, then, I should consult Him on how to spend my day.

Soap operas and other daytime television shows were immediately out—a waste of precious time. Even my husband thought they were ridiculous, though he had never asked me not to watch them. But as if the timing was right for my stubborn little spirit to be willing, he suggested that I no longer watch soap operas. I agreed, thinking there was much more I could do with my time, so I made a decision with him that I would never watch them.

But one day I seemed terribly bored, and I sheepishly turned the television on . . . just to see what was happening on "General Hospital." As my toddler and I were sitting on the floor in front of the TV, I heard a car pulling into the driveway. My husband, who rarely came home during the day, proceeded to walk through the front door. I dived for the knob, turned the TV off, ran to the radio, and pretended as if I had not been watching TV. Immediately, I sensed the deceit that I was going to be a part of if I continued this process. That little scenario was enough to convince me to never watch soap operas again.

Daydreaming about losing weight and inches was replaced with doing exercises, now a looked-forward-to physical release of anxieties and tensions rather than a dreaded discipline. Once again I seemed ready and willing *in spirit* to make a change in an area I had long desired to see disciplined, but had no motivation prior to my commitment to pray an hour a day.

Because my best friend from high school already had the discipline of regular exercise as a part of her life, our relationship rekindled, finding spiritual growth as well as companionship and accountability in our exercise schedule. She would pick me up for aerobics three times a week, or we'd exercise in our homes to a video. We counted on each other to be disciplined, yet maintained a personal inner drive to achieve our weight goals. Discipline was infiltrating every area of my life.

Motivational Christian radio shows—Dobson, Swindoll, and the like—filled the hours of my day instead of secular music or daytime television talk shows. Now, life with God was not only my occupation, but my preoccupation as well. The fire was burning once again!

Before long, it was apparent that prayer must come in the earliest part of my day, otherwise distractions, phone calls, laundry, even family members needing something to eat interrupted that quiet hour with God. Among other things, that meant no more sleeping in. Since I had an appointment to keep, it had to be planned for and put on the calendar. Had this appointment been with anyone else—friend, student, or businessperson—I would have had the same professional concerns and made the same courteous efforts of being on time, prepared, alert, and attentive. Therefore, I daily kept an "appointment" frame of mind in planning my hour with God. And on those inevitable days when things just didn't go as I had planned, the decision to pray an hour a day, made in that seminar room months earlier, kept me accountable. I either stayed up late or hid away during midday. I was determined!

More Immediate Results

Concerted prayer produced undeniable answers to specific requests, and this hour of prayer began within me a personal transformation producing such positive differences in my character and lifestyle that even my family noticed. Not only did I crack the dawn awaking often before my alarm and tiptoeing out of the bedroom rather than following my usual "hit the snooze three times for extra sleep" habit, but I held my temper in check with my toddler rather than become unreasonably angry.

Equally surprising, but perhaps not as pleasant, prayer uncovered personality flaws that had been swept under the rug, shoved aside, and denied for many years, revealing an escape artist's tactics in avoiding God's correction or conviction. But with daily prayer, what once seemed too painful or personal to deal with—a competitive jealousy toward others, visible, uncontrolled anger, and the firm grasp unforgiveness had upon my emotions—now was approachable. When I willingly exposed these flaws to a loving Father and over time disposed of them with His help, my friendships blossomed, unhealthy inclinations to compete and compare were either reproved or diminished, and my self-image vastly improved.

Prayer was no longer a drudgery that I considered boring or for the elderly; it was becoming an attainable, addicting, healing, spiritual discipline I had never taken time to pursue. Now I was cookin'!

Teach Me to Pray!

I had only scratched the surface of understanding more of the dynamics of prayer when an insatiable appetite for reading about the subject occurred. I began rummaging through shelves at my office and in our home, looking for books on prayer.

41

I found books on prayer I never realized I had and just *knew* I hadn't bought. I couldn't tell you where I had gotten them. That, to me, was not chance, but one more sign of God's hand prodding me, leading me to pray.

I discovered a thirty-year-old, yellow-paged classic by a long-gone, but greatly respected fellow, Andrew Murray, on the subject of prayer. One morning the title of his book, *The Prayer Life*, caught my eye. I slipped it from its row on a shelf beside my bed, where it must have been for years unnoticed, and leafed through the first, fifth, twentieth, then forty-fifth page. Before I realized it, I was sitting on the floor reading for over half an hour. Engrossed, I could hardly believe what I was reading.

Detailed in this old book was the account of his life renewed and empowered through the discovery of the power in prayer. He said the discipline of prayer was a most dynamic source of power for the believer, especially a minister, but one *most* neglected. I gasped as I recognized I had just walked through this book's journey! Even in the foreword I could see the similarity between my experience and Andrew Murray's experience of having been in ministry and seemingly powerless. He, along with other ministers in the year 1912 in South Africa, had discovered that prayerlessness was the deep-rooted problem resulting in a lack of spiritual power.

He wrote, "Prayer is in every deed the pulse of spiritual life. It is the great means of bringing to minister and people the blessing and power of heaven. Persevering and believing prayer means a strong and abundant life."

He went on to say that once the "spirit of confession began to prevail," meaning that once each individual confessed and repented of prayerlessness, it became possible to expect to gain the victory over all that in the past hindered the person's prayer life. The

South African ministers found that "a life in His love and fellowship will make prayer to Him the natural expression of our soul's life."

I, too, was finding a newness in my relationship with Jesus Christ that no longer would allow me to ignore the need for teaching from Christ Himself. Only He could give me the power to live how I knew I could and should live on this earth. Wow! "In spiritual work everything depends upon prayer and that God Himself is the helper of those who wait on Him." How long—all seven years?—had I lived without this power available to my life?

This little book described the journey of prayerlessness, the fight to overcome it, the new blessing of the victory over prayerlessness. Then it exhorted me with biblical examples of Jesus' prayer life and explained that the Holy Spirit was a prompter to pray and that the results of prayer in a believer's life would be obedience and powerful preaching. The benefits would be overflowing. It was incredible, exciting, and stirring.

But Andrew Murray wasn't the only one who had once neglected prayer. Peter Marshall, former chaplain of the Senate in the late forties, also resounded with the conviction that neglecting to pray was personal loss. He declared, "The whole field of prayer, and praying as laying hold on unlimited power, is unexplored, with the result that spiritual laws still lie undiscovered by the average believer." And he added that "sometimes, in our desperation, we hit upon the right way to pray, and things happen—our prayers are gloriously answered. But for the most part, our praying is very haphazard, and the results are often disappointing."

It wasn't long before I was soaking up antiquated books on prayer, which motivated me toward the lost art of my generation (at least an art not much discussed or excitedly taught!). And without fail, I would uncover hidden treasures in poignant quotes and phrases, such as "Neglect prayer. Neglect God," by O. Hallesby, in-

43

creasing my firm determination to cling to a daily appointment with God.

As if my eyes were blinded, then suddenly opened, I realized that prayer was essential for a Christian to practice. Once again and with childlike delight, I was making Jesus my constant companion, One I could talk to, cry with, complain to, or seek advice from. I learned *not* to wish or worry, but to simply pray!

In my daily hour of quiet time with the Lord, writing my conversations, listening for His response, and reading His Word, a new strength was developing. I would encounter God in a new way, discover something fresh about His character daily, and receive a boldness to believe Him for more and more power in my life. I found a boldness once again living within me to evangelize while standing at the checkout counter in the grocery store, while talking to the postman, while coaching at the local high school, while being in any situation. Each moment of my life seemed to have a purpose. I would ask myself, *What would Jesus have me do right now? What would He have me say?* I didn't feel timid or directionless or weak.

But inevitably, by the end of each day, I sensed my spirit needing renewal, exhortation, and direction. And as weak as I would come to our daily appointment, I would leave twice as strong and with a deep desire to pull others toward Him.

Hour after hour revealed that God was not *just* real or *just* alive, but intimately involved and interested in every circumstance of one's day. I was inclined to change plans, turn down one road versus another, rethink through my day, decide how to make the most use of every hour, and even look for God's hand in interruptions, asking Him how I should deal with them rather than get frustrated over them.

In that hour I would receive the detailed directions for each day—God's plan and the promise of His Holy Spirit's power to guide me. "Marching orders," as Peter

Marshall called God's specific will for one's daily life, created great excitement that could be evidenced by many! Phone calls long awaited would ring in, ministry and business decisions snapped into place, and I would constantly whisper to myself, "He did it. Just as He said. Just as He promised." And the more answers to prayer, change of circumstances, healings, and mended relationships that would unfold, the more vocal I became about my daily appointment with God.

"I've Gotta Tell Everyone"

At first people would just humor me, thinking my childlike faith was "cute." But with each passing day and "you won't believe what God did" story, their expressions and questions grew more serious.

"You don't really pray for one hour, do you?"

"That was just a coincidence, don't you think?"

"Maybe you shouldn't tell so many people you pray an hour a day. That sounds too pious."

But soon, it was, "Umm, Becky, would you pray for me? My . . ."

Even my relationship with my husband and God became more of a threesome. Roger had taught me to write my prayers as a young Christian, and he had daily practiced what he preached through all the years of our marriage by journalizing his prayers. Therefore, when I made such a radical time commitment to pray, he watched with interest as each day passed. Because I was so sensitive now to God's voice, I would say, "God spoke to me," and he cautioned me, suggesting that I say, "I feel that God is saying to me . . ." His wise advice allowed me the freedom to practice listening to God and sometimes fail, and it also allowed me to be corrected and accountable to others whom God had put in my life as mentors, adding credibility to my accounts of conversations with God.

In listening to God's voice, we felt that His counsel

45

to us as individuals would be similar. If there was ever a discrepancy, we would continue seeking God until Roger and I both felt Him saying the *same thing* to us (in relationship to ministry, family, or our future). We would continue to look for scriptural confirmation or additional circumstances or wait for the Holy Spirit to sway one of us—to make a unanimous decision of three!

One such time was shortly after the birth of our son, Jacob. Roger felt God wanted us to have another child. I had barely recovered from the aftereffects of a tough delivery, and I panicked. At that point, he and I differed dramatically on what God was saying to us.

Since we had reached an impasse, I suggested we make an appointment with our pastor, though that in itself seemed like risky living because our pastor had nine children. But after hearing us out and praying with us, our pastor suggested that, because of my high level of anxiety, immediately pursuing childbearing would not be in the best interest of our marriage and friendship. Relieved and feeling God's direction and comfort through our pastor, we put the issue on hold and regularly brought it up for reconsideration.

Within a few short months, prayer was noticeably changing every facet of my life *and* releasing the power of God that was both undeniable and appealing. Reading and rereading Andrew Murray's many books on prayer unveiled the words, "Prayer is the secret of power and life. Not only for ourselves, but for others, for the church, for the world, it is to prayer that God has given the right to take hold of Him and His strength. It is on prayer that the promises wait for their fulfillment." Not only was I *learning* to pray, but I was changing by praying!

Change Your Priorities, Possibilities, Personality, and Perspectives Through Prayer

Priorities

Perhaps the most obvious side effect of a daily appointment with the Lord was the fact that it found its way into a packed schedule. The once-hectic lifestyle of car-pool mom, youth worker, cheerleading coach, and housewife found an anchor by beginning each day with an hour of written prayer. This Type A, near hyperactive woman was forced to change her priorities *if* she was going to walk her talk.

It became a conscious commitment to pencil onto my calendar the time each day that I was going to have my quiet time. In planning my business day (aerobics, lunch appointments, business and ministry meetings, or social events), I was no longer looking for time with God; I was *making* time for God. How true the statement became, "If you don't have time for God, you don't have time!" But it was more; I was *learning* to give God time. As Andrew Murray said, "God needs time with us. If we would only give Him time . . . to exercise the full influence of His presence on us."

His presence through the Word and times in prayer *goaded me* to change a negative attitude when I was stubborn or to release an unmet expectation or disappointment, *motivated me* when I was procrastinating to complete a promise or confront a difficult situation, and *guided me* with ideas, creativity, and direction in short- and long-term projects.

My appointments with God were definitely
    changing my priorities,
        pushing away the clutter, and
            revealing the difference between
                the urgent and the important.

I changed from failing to plan and not seeing *any* results to being an organized planner of my time and accomplishing goals. Planning, goal setting, and time management suddenly became subjects of great interest to me. Why? Because time in conversation with God produced ideas that seemed reachable and exciting. They had God-confidence behind them. But would I sit there each morning and just dwell on those thoughts as something that "could be," or would I take those ideas as implanted within me by God to be acted upon?

Initially I would hear God speak to me about relationships. I had a Christian friend who was getting psychiatric counseling. I didn't know how I could help, and I would avoid the thought that God wanted me to do something until it grew loud and clear. As if I could not ignore God's prodding any longer, I felt I needed to extend a visual expression of my love and concern for my friend. The idea came in my quiet time one morning to send flowers to my friend, which was not at all my usual method of encouragement nor an item in the budget. I asked my husband what he thought of sending a cheery bouquet of flowers to our mutual, hurting friend. His immediate agreement signaled to both of us that, though out of the ordinary, this idea seemed God-inspired, and we should gladly proceed. When our friend called that afternoon, we could almost see the smile on her face and hear the joy that had been missing in her voice for weeks!

That was just the start of what "giving" ideas would come out of time in prayer. Though we had been tithers since our wedding day, I always seemed to give—no more, no less than 10 percent—with reservation and without a willing spirit.

One Christmas, my prayers focused on giving *cheerfully*. Why couldn't I? Why didn't I? Why did I find the act of giving so difficult? I had assumed that the spiritual gift of giving was not a gift I possessed; therefore, I was inclined to give out of duty. But that way of thinking was getting battered down and beaten like waves on a shore eroding the bank as the Word of God washed through my daily thoughts and caused me to examine my motives.

I purposed to change that area of my life. Then, as always, when the spirit within me was willing to change, an opportunity arose for me to act upon.

We put our house up for sale a few months after I developed the desire to become a cheerful giver. It was at the same time that a Jamaican missionary wanted desperately to attend the Billy Graham Evangelists Conference in Europe. He did not have any money and did not know anyone who could financially help him, except for me, because I had been his small group leader in Youth For Christ years earlier.

When my missionary friend boldly asked me for five hundred dollars (which I did not have), it appeared more than likely that God prodded him to call upon me, providing me with an opportunity to stretch my faith, give willingly, and obey Him. In addition, he needed the money by a certain date. In faith I believed that we would certainly sell our house by the time he needed the money. Without thinking of the consequences or even consulting my husband about how much we would sell our house for or how much profit would be made, I told my Jamaican friend that I would send him

10 percent of the earnings from the sale of our house in time for him to attend the Billy Graham Conference.

After I hung up the phone, I asked my husband if that was okay. He looked at me with one of those looks that only a husband can give after a wife has put her foot in her mouth and said, "I guess it's going to have to be." At that point I got down on my knees and asked God if He would quickly sell our house. I told Him we would give 10 percent of our earnings to our friend who needed it by that summer. It was exactly 10 percent of our profit, when all was said and done, that I sent in the knick of time for our Jamaican friend to attend the conference in Europe! That experience was a turning point in trusting God to arrange the priorities of my life. I was certainly stretched to believe that I could be a cheerful giver and that God would help me in the process.

The two went hand in hand—time in prayer led to action steps that needed to be carried out in a disciplined fashion unto completion. Calendars, lists, phone calls, and correspondence—*all* needed to be included in a day's work where previously watching television, telephoning, and pursuing other time wasters had achieved little for the kingdom of God.

Becky, Know Your "Call"!

As my renewed priorities fell into place, my life's purpose gained shape. I could see, pray for, and take daily steps toward achieving what I hoped for and what I could not see but looked forward to with complete assurance and inner conviction. The priorities once placed on luncheons, work, leisure, worship, and sleep all needed reevaluating and adjusting *because* of prayer. At one time I would say yes to almost every request, but now, when an opportunity arose, an interruption occurred, or a door opened, I weighed its importance on the basis of my personal call in life as wife, mom, youth worker, writer, speaker, then I *prayer-*

fully considered its priority before making a decision. The more I'd make wrong choices, the more quickly I learned to make the right choices for use of my time. Overbooking a calendar day with too much activity, saying yes too often to "the good but not the best," not meeting deadlines, and being late for appointments because I miscalculated driving times or answered the phone when I shouldn't have were painful and sometimes humiliating lessons, but their sting caused me to increase my awareness of God's plan for my daily life in relationship to my life's purpose and often pushed me into another timely transition. The outcome? Decisions came more easily, and responses to requests came more rapidly. My ability to discern God's will for my life grew sharper.

Little did I know what I was asking for when I made a simple decision to pray for an hour each day!

After recognizing the disorganized lifestyle I had been maintaining and groping my way back to a healthier, more disciplined condition, I discovered excellent tools for speedy recovery and growth. Guiding me to evaluate and manage my time were experts such as Anne Ortlund in *Disciplines of the Beautiful Woman,* Ted Engstrom with *The Pursuit of Excellence,* and Gordon MacDonald's *Ordering Your Private World.* In MacDonald's "memo to the disorganized" it almost seemed as simple as this: "If my private world is in order, it will be because I'm convinced that the inner world of the spiritual must govern the outer world of activity." I came to believe that time is important to God and godly use of time should be important to the believer. How are we to live every day if we don't consult the Spirit of God to give us wisdom, affirmation, encouragement, direction, and guidance in place of the world's noise, confusion, and disorganization?

In *Ordering Your Private World* I discovered a description of a life lived out of prayer: "Finally at the center we are filled by the power and strength of God as

51

Holy Spirit. There is a resurgence of confidence and expectancy. We receive insight and wisdom; faith that removes mountains is generated, and our love for others, even for the unloveable, begins to grow." Isn't that what it is all about? The books thoroughly convinced me that a Christian's every hour is valuable to God, and they equally convinced me that wasting time was certainly an expensive and *inexcusable* loss of time for the kingdom!

Possibilities

As my priorities realigned themselves, my vision cleared and I could see forever! Time with God proved invaluable in the area of dreaming big dreams and believing that with God's help they were possible, even though (especially as a former alcoholic) a shadow of the past tended to shade any self-confidence and adventuresome spirit that dared to dream. Nevertheless, having lacked the necessary discipline for turning dreams into reality *prior* to my hour meetings with God, I was astonished at a newfound sense of determination and endurance to achieve what once seemed improbable or impossible.

Over and over again, I would have the idea to speak at an event, meet a person, visit a special place, or even turn my spoken testimony into an article—even a book! And for as many times as I would shove the idea aside, it would return. I then heard a pastor share, "If an idea doesn't go away, begin to treat it as if it is from God. Let *Him* bring it to pass." My appointments with God often contained conversations
    that turned into hopes,
        then became goals that structured plans
            and ultimately turned into accomplishments.
I even surprised myself with the action steps I would take to see a dream fulfilled, especially when the odds were stacked against me. Once, in a conversation

with a distributor, I was told no to an idea simply because of having no previous track record in sales.

If the distributor would accept my product, I had an offer from a large company to sell my product—beginning with a (large for me) minimum order of 350. Seeing this immediate opportunity falling apart in front of me, I basically said to the fellow on the other end of the line whom I'd never met, "You can't say no." He said, "Lady, you don't have a track record." I said, "What's a track record?" He remarked, "Proven sales." I said, "But I just sold 500 in two months! Isn't that enough?" He said, "Well, not for a national distributor." I said, "If you say no to me, I will not have an opportunity to fill this order. You just can't say no. You have to give me a chance." Then slowly and with reservation he asked, "Lady, how much is each unit?" We made an initial agreement that he would order 350, and within two months he had ordered an additional 1,000 books.

From the thought to call a person or to suggest a direction in a meeting or to send a manuscript to a publisher, my possibilities became realities, and my faith was constantly stretched to step out into new areas of trust in God.

Scriptures on faith increased the assuredness that this recent result of time with God (dreaming!) was not unusual activity, but one that had been lying dormant just waiting to be released. Instead of being timid or insecure that these ideas—some *looking* impossible—were not from God, I adopted more of the "Philippians 4" attitude: "I can do all things through Christ who strengthens me." And though initially I may have looked foolish or even arrogant to dream big dreams, I sensed God's assuredness filling me.

As days and weeks and even months would pass without an outward sign I was indeed moving in *God's* direction, I would cling to the Word and my faith, fueled by the Holy Spirit's conviction that what I believed

God had planned for my life would indeed come to pass. I sometimes felt ridiculous—like Noah with on-lookers smirking at my eccentric faith. At other times I was indignant—like Jonah thinking, *Why do I have to do this?* And I often felt abandoned—like Joseph in a prison—because of telling others the "dream" I believed God had given me.

Yet, *always*, God's answers came through in His time, whisking me even more confidently into another adventure with Him. Because He had proven His faithfulness through innumerable circumstances, dreaming God's possibilities became my regular practice. A one-time daydreamer, I was now a dreamer determined to follow through each day with God's plan—definitely a new fruit of my daily time in prayer.

Personality

Weak, insecure, easily angered, jealous, selfish, and *lazy* were all words that described my personality prior to hourly appointments with God. Not that those negative qualities vanished forever, but I possessed a new and strong censorship of those characteristics by the Holy Spirit within me. It was not only temper outbursts, cold looks, or an outer hardness that faded, but what once seemed semi-acceptable behavior for a Christian (cutting remarks, mild gossip, or loose slang) now elicited a holy poke from within me. Through the years following my conversion, I reverted to many "old nature" habits or manipulation, moodiness, harbored resentments, bitterness, and jealousies. Not long after I had allowed the discipline of prayer to affect my day, I was confronted (almost bombarded) with my sickly inner life—one needing sanctification. Many hours of prayer revealed much sin, and lots of tears and endless conversations with God brought about confession and ultimately restoration.

Since my conversion experience in 1976, I had been fully aware of the Holy Spirit's power, gifts, and manifestations, but I had not consciously invited the person of the Holy Spirit into my daily walk for years. Now my renewed belief in Him as a powerful person within me, rather than a ghostly entity floating about haphazardly, prompted me to call upon Him and submit to His available strength and power.

As if I had lost touch with a close friend, I felt remorse at my stupidity and ignorance of leaving Him out of my life. I became quicker to sense sin in my thought life—doubts, malice, envy, or jealousy—and the Spirit and my "flesh" came often to war.

No longer could I casually speed without noticing the speedometer; I'd feel the blush of red cheeks that accompanies doing something wrong, and then I'd tap on the brakes. I could no longer relate something to a friend and conveniently omit a fact that would embarrass me because an immediate guilty verdict would pound in my ears. For instance, if I had forgotten to give someone a message that I was responsible for relaying, I could no longer say, "Oh, I couldn't get hold of that person," or make up an excuse because the spirit within me would bring the truth quickly to my mind so that I had to speak it. I could no longer spank my son out of anger without sensing that I was just as wrong in the situation by being out of control as an adult. I was even caught by a principal who said to me, "Well, how many missed the practice?" when I had exaggerated by saying, "Everyone missed the practice." I realized that I needed to speak the truth at all times.

Not only my mouth, but my "eyes" were under scrutiny. I would feel a dull pain in my stomach when I watched a movie or television show that would elicit strong memories of my old life . . . the sensual, fast-paced lifestyle of young Americans today. I could no longer watch certain TV programs without dwelling on

55

them in my thought life, and they spurred within me an immediate contradiction of what time with God had shown me.

Slowly, the Spirit began to gain the upper hand and control the "flesh" within me as long as I would
acknowledge,
call upon, and
daily request the Holy Spirit's empowering
and indwelling of my person.
Though the action was obviously supernatural and invisible, I chose to believe the Holy Spirit was transforming my personality, and I consciously asked Him to do so daily in prayer.

The result? Many hidden and obvious habits and flaws surfaced in my life, received inner healing, then came under the control of the Spirit and eventually were flushed out. I was daily being refined, confronted, confessed, and forgiven through prayer. A newer, softer person was emerging after each appointment with God.

Perspectives

Not only did prayer and its phenomenal results cause my perspective of prayer to drastically change, but my perspective of God truly changed as well.

Not that I hadn't felt God's love *toward me*, but an emotional love *toward Him* was developing as a result of my time in prayer. How could it be any different? Spending so much time together—with anyone— developed a solid friendship and trust. And within that relationship, God never ceased to amaze me, nor did He ever disappoint me. Oh, I was disappointed in *my* unmet expectations when I would infringe upon His character by *telling* Him how or when to answer a prayer rather than *asking* Him to meet my needs, but nothing He ever promised did He withdraw from or fail to perform. His unfailing love and faithful, loyal character became a strength to me, which I wanted to be around as often as possible, and He continually proved His trust-worthiness through daily intervention. He was gentle and comforting when I failed or needed help, and in starting over, I would want to know His will and would ask Him to show me.

Each transition in my life seemed heralded by a trumpeter when a circumstance would occur to change the course of my life or when I would meet a new friend or bump into a perfect stranger who would become the missing piece in the puzzle of my life.

Once while I was sitting in a youth workers' training retreat, a guest speaker nonchalantly mentioned an organization she was affiliated with—C.L.A.S.S. (Christian Leaders and Speakers Seminars). The mere mention of the name C.L.A.S.S. (unrelated to her purpose in being there) triggered something within me to find out much more because I had been daily asking God to give me the skills to speak the message of my testimony. I requested a brief appointment with the speaker, and upon returning home from the retreat, I immediately followed up on the whereabouts of the next and nearest C.L.A.S.S. That "coincidence" resulted in training, traveling, and a teacher-mentor relationship with Florence and Fred Littauer, founders of C.L.A.S.S. and authors of numerous Christian books.

Another time, I had been daily asking the Lord to open doors for me to speak to young people. Having relocated, I was so new to the West Coast of the United States that I hardly knew where to begin to build contacts. Attending a National Youth Workers Convention in San Francisco seemed a good beginning, but anonymity in a large convention hall was overwhelming. In the very last hour of the convention I clumsily bumped into the cofounder of Youth Specialties, Mike Yaconelli, and that initial, spontaneous conversation resulted in consecutive years of speaking opportunities to teens and youth workers.

I realized I knew no Other who knew me so well

and still loved me so much! I came to see God not as a distant God but as an ever-so-present Friend and Father.

I learned that prayer is not a monologue to a deaf God, but a conversation with a God who hears prayer.

Prayer is not helping God with an answer; it is asking God to help. It is not telling God what to do; it is telling Him my needs. It isn't so much for the disciplined as for the undisciplined!

Prayer is not necessarily meant to be an easy joy ride, but it definitely is a spiritual discipline that produces joy!

Prayer is not *just* coming to Jesus; it is letting Jesus come into me!

Prayer is not only for the educated, seminary scholar; it is for anyone who will practice, persevere, and plan to pray!

Prayer is *not* a substitute for time in the Word; it will lead *to* the Word.

Prayer is not for the impatient, but for the one who waits!

Prayer is not a place to boast, but a place to confess. Prayer is not my motivating God, but God's motivating me.

Prayer is *not* a waste of time; it is an appointment with the King of kings!

My perspective of prayer *and* God changed!

The initial discovery months earlier that power is released when one prays and that prayerlessness is sin prompted me to make a nonnegotiable, no-turning-back decision to pray for one hour a day. After the decision had become a daily discipline, affecting every area of my life, I needed desperately to get that hour of prayer organized so that I could be, as James 5:16 stated, a righteous and effective pray-er, availing much!

How to Pray
the "Write" Way

I found out the hard way that to be a successful
pray-er I needed to
prepare my heart for prayer,
plan my time in prayer, and
practice the art of prayer.

Prepare Your Heart

Have an attitude of anticipation.

Every morning, it is extremely helpful to picture
yourself looking forward to actually meeting with the
person of Jesus Christ. To imagine Him sitting across
the table, grasping your hand or touching you comfort-
ingly upon your shoulder, wiping a tear, smiling
warmly, laughing softly, or raising His eyebrows at
your suggestions personalizes your appointment with
God.

He is a person! Perhaps it is because of our misconceptions of Him as apart from us, *in* heaven, or as an
entity, unfamiliar and distant, that we awkwardly initiate transcendental thoughts that bounce out to no-
where or within the four walls of a room to no one.

To prepare your heart for prayer is to *expect* His

presence in your meeting, to wait in expectation for Him and His responses as David modeled in his conversations of prayer. Surely he was expressing, crying, and appealing to no one less than a person in much of the book of Psalms, his quiet time journal. David was so personal and intimate with his God. And why should you come with any less an attitude of expectancy that God will meet you, hear you, or answer you?

Not to expect anything from time with God just may be exactly what will occur, and soon time with God will become a tedious discipline. But anticipate throughout each day the new revelations, the increased faith, and the heart's desires awaiting you in your next appointment with God, and He will not—cannot—disappoint you.

Why "Abide in Him" Daily?

John 15, the chapter where Jesus discusses with His disciples the vine and branches, seems truly to be about spending time with God—what it reaps *and* that it is His request of those who call themselves His disciples. In different New Testament versions, the key phrase is either "abide" or "remain in Me." If you replace either of those phrases with "spend time with Me," you have the following reasons for having a regular, daily appointment with God:

1. If you spend time with God, He will spend time with you (v. 4).
2. You *cannot* bear fruit unless you spend time with God (v. 4).
3. But you will bear much fruit if you spend time with Him (v. 5).
4. Anyone who does not spend time with God will be thrown away like a branch, picked up, thrown into the fire, and burned (v. 6).
5. If you spend time with Him and His words spend time in you, "Ask whatever you wish, and it will be given you" (v. 7).

6. Now spend time basking in God's love (v. 9)!

It appears clear that Jesus wants us:

- To spend time with Him for the furtherance of His kingdom.
- To receive His love.
- To be empowered to do His works.
- To know Him and His ways so intimately that whatever we ask will be given to us!

In that light, is asking God selfish, requesting prayer, or is it answers to prayer resulting from fully knowing God *and* His will for your life because you have spent time with Him daily?

Doesn't it work that way in your closest relationships? You know their personality, their preferences, and their precepts, and you rarely overstep, infringe, or misread them because you know a lot about them before you ask of them. That is the result of spending time with God as well!

Plan Your Start: Have a Plan to Abide

If you've cleared up the issues of *who* you are meeting and *why,* then *where, when,* and *how* to have a successful quiet time are the next most helpful questions to ask yourself.

Where?

Have a familiar place to meet with God daily—out in the yard, at the breakfast table, at your office desk, by the garden window, or even by the fireplace. Set the atmosphere with either complete silence or soft, instrumental music. The discipline of meeting in the same place develops a consistent pattern.

For best results, ask yourself where will you be least interrupted and most comfortable for a specific period of time, then make that your place for a quiet time.

61

When?

I found, ideally, morning hours afforded quiet, uninterrupted time with God—before the phone rang and duty or responsibility called. Earlier on some days than others, my appointment with God increased my awareness of His plan for the day ahead of me, giving God the opportunity to influence my decisions and choices for the coming day and allowing me to get the renewed, fresh start that confession and forgiveness offer. My research proved that the "morning watch," as Andrew Murray called his time with God (though any time of the day is appropriate), was the earliest hour, before a day's work had begun and the time most often suggested by godly persons in the Bible and in personal biographies.

How?

Choose a *specific* amount of time that will be your minimum standard appointment. Though this could tend to sound legalistic, the accountability of a set amount of time allows you to plan realistically for your appointment with God and increases the probability of your actually keeping the appointment. The structure of a time block prompts you to set an alarm earlier, go to bed earlier, or excuse yourself if necessary in order to protect your time with God.

My personal experience proved that when life got inevitably and unusually busy or I was out of town or on vacation, no set time dwindled down to no time with God at all. And when I had extra time, it was always a pleasure to have leisurely, increased appointments with God. I was confident and comfortable that in setting a specific amount of time—an amount I considered fully sufficient to encompass all aspects of my relationship with Him (confession, intercession, Bible reading, etc.)—I would be successful in my commitment. It was not a burden, but a blessing!

Practice Your Part

Practice, practice, practice.

Written prayer was a transcript of my conversations with God. I could look back and review a day or a week or a year in my journey with God. I learned to pray specifically, with perseverance, hope, and faith. I could retrace times when I thought God was not answering a prayer only to see it as a delay and not a denial. I could review the course of a prayer request—its evolution from where it started, how my desires changed (or *were* changed by God), and how its final answer was always timely, exciting, and often exhilarating.

Practicing prayer, like any sport or discipline, took
- Time and effort
- A practice schedule
- Regular review and evaluation
- Variety added into my training program
- Additional training on a regular basis
- Built-in accountability factors
- Goals
- A reward program

Prayer became such an integral part of my daily life that I didn't realize I was progressing through stages of learner, intermediate, and advanced, much like on the ski slopes. Yet, practice, like skiing, included risk taking—some big spills and lots of chills and thrills. With practice and instructions from my private Tutor I would go from

fear to faith,
doubt to trust, and
intimidation to boldness.

It aroused a competitive edge within me to become an excellent pray-er, to make prayer a discipline that I loved. Written prayer kept my appointments with God alive, personal, conversational, spontaneous, emotional, and adventuresome!

63

PART III

■

The Design
for Prayer

One Christian's Secret to a Happy Hour

Three months after I had made the decision to pray for an hour a day and had mastered the discipline by writing my prayers and recording God's responses, I knew I needed a sense of order.

For quite a few years I had attended church regularly on Sunday morning, but had dashed home in order to watch "The Hour of Power," Robert Schuller's Sunday morning church service. I always took notes and often counted on his weekly message for motivation. *Weekly* I felt God used Dr. Schuller's sermons to fuel my faith and encourage me to believe that—though I was "only a housewife" and part-time youth worker— God had put a dream in my heart and a message in my mouth and somehow, someday, would have a plan to use them for His glory.

One Monday morning, after a particularly motivational "Hour of Power" church service the day before, I stared out my kitchen window while seated at my regular quiet time spot with pen, paper, highlighter, and Bible. It was still dark outside, and I almost hoped for Jesus to walk up the sidewalk and join me for coffee and toast. Some days I would ache for the touch of His hand and the sound of His voice by saying, "Couldn't

You just come here and show and tell me exactly what to do?" My present dilemma was in relationship to my hour of prayer.

I needed a plan. I needed accountability and organization. I said, "How does Robert Schuller get all these great ideas—'turn your scars into stars,' 'inch by inch anything's a cinch'?"

As if spoken by God in response to my comment (or was it a complaint?), James 4:2 came to my mind: "You do not have, because you do not ask God." So I did.

"Lord," I wrote, "You always give Robert Schuller these great ideas. Could You give me just one?"

I should have known *then* to take God at His word, for the next conversation that took place between us resulted in dreaming, designing, ordering, speaking, forming a small business, and selling over fourteen thousand notebooks within the following few years— and the potential and probability of distributing many more!

God had given me an idea. It came like gushing water released from a pipe that had broken loose. My pen wrote as fast as the thoughts and ideas came, leaving little room for inquiries of my own to interrupt God's thoughts to me:

> Develop a notebook, a three-ring binder, call it *My Partner*, use it each morning, carry it to church, and consider it a complement to your Bible. It will have two PARTs— yours and Mine.

MY PART of the notebook would have four sections, P.A.R.T., a place to journalize my prayers. The first section, PRAISE, was devotional reading, studying, and praying by reading four to five psalms a day and rewriting them as my personal praise prayers. It opened up the Word—and my heart—at the start of each appointment with God.

In the next section, ADMIT, I honestly discussed

my temper, my impatience, and other missed marks with the One who already knew them, but was waiting for my agreement with Him and my confession to Him. I had gained an assurance by meeting with God every day that integrity, blamelessness, and holiness were *assets* in the life of a believer, not cursed burdens of effort, but characteristics I should be striving for. I wrote daily the words of Psalm 139:23–24 and left my ADMIT section lifted by the promise of Romans 12:2 that His Holy Spirit was daily renewing my mind.

Psalm 5:3 described the third section, REQUESTS:

> In the morning, O LORD, you hear my voice;
>   in the morning I lay my requests before you
>   and wait in expectation.

Each morning I laid my requests before God and waited expectantly for His reply, aware that "a request may or may not be granted"—as reminded by C. S. Lewis. Most of all, the dynamics of prayer requests held great potential for my faith to mature.

Finally, the THANKS section was where I daily acknowledged to God that I recognized His touch, His love, and His intimacy in my life through all the circumstances, interventions, and answers to specific requests arranged by His hand. MY PART of *My Partner* took me one hour. Could it be a coincidence? Surely not in my mind!

GOD'S PART to me came in the form of an acrostic as well—L.M.N.O.P. "L" was the section of my notebook specifically set aside for planned times of silent LISTENING to God. "M" was the MESSAGES section, where I would take notes of sermons, outlines, and Scripture verses shared by my pastor. And "N.O.P." held paper for recording verses from the NEW and OLD TESTAMENTS and the book of PROVERBS that either comforted or convicted me. The last tab in the notebook, making ten sections, was labeled "TO DO."

REQUESTS

Ask and it will be given to you; seek and you will find; knock and the door will be opened to you. For everyone who asks receives; he who seeks finds; and to him who knocks, the door will be opened. Matthew 7:7, 8

There are a number of Scripture verses like Matthew 7:7, 8 that encourage you, the believer, to ask God for his plan and will for your life. Philippians 4:6 invites you to pray about everything, rather than to worry! When you think about it, what can worry ever change, add, or take away from a situation? Matthew 6:31-34 shows how many of us worry about things like clothes, food, and drink. In verse 33, Jesus says, "But seek first his kingdom and his righteousness, and all these things will be given to you as well."

What does it mean to "seek God first"? It means to look for, search, and pursue him and his will for your life. And what better way to search for his will than through a daily prayer time and consistent devotional life?

God wants us to ask him for his will. In James 4:2 we read, "You do not have, because you do not ask God." Wow! Try putting into practice the simple principle of asking for God's will for one week, then record the results. You will be amazed to see how specifically God answers your prayers!

When I am praying about my hopes and dreams, Psalm 37:4 comes to mind: "Delight yourself in the Lord and he will give you the desires of your heart." Take a moment to think about what it means for you to "delight yourself in the Lord."

I cannot stress enough how much God wants to bless your life through answered prayer. He desires to meet your every need (Phil. 4:19) and direct your every path (Prov. 3:5, 6)!

If you want to know God's perfect will for your life, you must *ask* him for it. Remember, once you ask you must be willing to wait for his timing, trust that he has it all in control, and obey what you believe he has told you. (If "knowing God's will" is something you are unsure of, be sure to take extra time to study verses in your Bible on that subject, or ask a pastor, parent, or local Christian bookstore for additional resources to help you understand it.)

TRY IT! APPLY IT!

This section, REQUESTS, will be one in which you write the most. Once you begin to talk to God about all of *your* needs, desires, and dreams, you'll need another page to talk to him about your family and friends, as well as world needs (such as hunger, missing children, and politics).

In order to *remember* to be diligent to pray for those who have asked you to pray for them and for those you want to pray for daily, a PRAYER LIST is an ideal way to spend time in this section. Depending on your time and ability to concentrate in prayer, make your list as detailed as fits your personality. Perhaps you will list all your family members by name and include a little phrase by each of their names. Next, you might list your personal plans for which you are seeking God's guidance. A section for those who are in need of physical or emotional healing may be appropriate for your prayer list. Include in your list the President and others in government who need safety, protection, and wisdom from God. Remember to pray for those who are without food (e.g., in Africa) and the organizations that are helping to meet their needs physically and spiritually. Add missionaries and pastors and others in ministry who touch your life. You will be amazed to watch your heart grow in concern and love for others as you pray daily for them.

After you have prayed through your daily PRAYER LIST, ask God to direct your day—your plans, your words, your steps. Colossians 1:9-12 is an *excellent* passage to turn into a prayer for yourself and others on a daily basis. I have experienced miraculous changes and circumstances as a result of this Scripture. Pray it for yourself!

I firmly believe that God *wants* us to *ask* him for his direction for our lives—now and for the future. James 4:2 says, "You do not have, because you do not ask God." How exciting it is to watch God *answer* your every prayer, especially when you have been diligent to ask him for his will and have waited on his answer! (God *always* answers the prayers of his children, but it may not always be with a "Yes." "No" and "Wait" are answers, too!) You have really begun to trust in him when you are open to his answer and timing for your requests.

NOW, YOU TRY IT and, in faith, expect results!

Morning by morning, O Lord, you hear my voice; morning by morning I lay my requests before you and wait in expectation. Psalm 5:3

LISTENING

The Lord confides in those who fear him; he makes his covenant known to them. Psalm 25:14

The area of spiritual discipline called listening to God is one of continual growth for all Christians. Believe it or not, it takes practice to hear God's voice! In fact, younger Christians may not feel adventurous in pursuing this section, but wise and godly counsel from a pastor or parent and the Word of God will encourage you in the practice of listening to God.

This section can be most difficult because it may be questionable whether *God* is speaking to you. You may wonder if the thoughts you are thinking are simply your own.

Even though some doubt may exist, quiet yourself before the Lord and record what you feel he is saying to you. "Be still, and know that I am God" (Ps. 46:10).

Listening to the voice of God comes with some practice and discernment. Knowing God's voice often comes with trial and error in the beginning. We hear instruction in our thoughts, such as, "Don't do this," or "Do that." If we follow the voice and find that it leads us astray, we realize that we listened to our own lusts, or perhaps even the enemy's tempting lure to sin. It is not long, however, before we know the Shepherd's voice. Listening to God can come in a planned moment, as you quiet yourself before God, meditate on his Word, ask him to reveal to you his thoughts and plans, and wait to hear his voice.

God may also speak through others—Christian friends, pastors, speakers, or books. Ask God each day to help you hear his voice.

TRY IT! APPLY IT!

Begin this section with a silent or written prayer, asking God to speak to you by his Holy Spirit. Be specific in asking about your needs and decisions, and ask if he has any direction for you. Be silent, attentive to the next thoughts that cross through your mind.

Many times a Scripture verse will come to mind. Write it down, then look up the reference if you don't know where it is. Turn to that verse and read the other verses before and after it. Look for verses that have direct implication to the prayers you have previously prayed in your PRAISE, ADMIT, REQUESTS, and THANKS sections. Very often I am either encouraged, comforted, corrected, or directed by what has come to mind and what I have read to follow it up. Once, concerned about a move, the passage in John 14 about God's peace came to my mind. I had been somewhat anxious about where we were going to live. When I came to verse 2, "I am going there to prepare a place for you," my heart jumped with excitement and I wrote the verse down in my LISTENING section. That afternoon, a gentleman whom I had never met called and asked if our family would house-sit for him for three months!

On another occasion, I felt that God was telling me to watch my driving. I wrote the phrase down in my LISTENING section . . . and two hours later I got a sixty-dollar ticket. I have taken my LISTENING section more seriously from that moment on! And I haven't gotten any more tickets! Many times in my LISTENING section I have experienced the *hope* in the Word of God come to reality in my life. It is not every day, but I wait and watch and ask him for those words of encouragement and direction in my life.

God might call you by name or speak to you about doing something for someone. You may feel led to pray for another person whose need he brings to your mind. The more time you spend listening to God, the easier it will become to hear him and get to know his voice. You may want to begin with only a few minutes of silent listening and then allow your time with him gradually to increase. Write down what you feel he is saying to you.

LISTENING

My Partner Prayer Notebook

The Tool: *My Partner Prayer Notebook*

Hours in prayer caused me to examine what was really happening when I prayed. What were the scriptural principles behind the results I was experiencing? What were the limits involved in asking of God? Who was privileged enough to receive God's listening ear? And how did the Word fit in so critically to one's time in prayer?

Answers came by simply following *My Partner*'s format of

- *P*raising God for who He is
- *A*dmitting my sins to Him on a daily basis
- *R*equesting of Him and believing that He hears and answers
- *T*hanking God daily for everything

And by

- *L*istening to Him and not talking, but recording
- *M*essages from Him through my pastor's sermons
- *N*ew Testament readings for understanding God through Jesus' life

- *O*ld Testament readings for understanding God through the history of the Jews
- *P*roverbs study to keep me on my toes

My Part

Praise

The **PRAISE** section began each daily appointment as personal praise prayers to God. At first, it was an awkward section. Knowing how to sing praises to God, but not knowing how to write them, led me to the book of Psalms for inspiration for my praise prayers. From the psalmists I discovered so much about God's character—His unfailing love, His constant care, His surrounding presence, and His invincible might and awesome power.

Through the words of praise in the psalms I learned to fear God, not be afraid of Him, but respect and reverence Him. There was every reason to fear God, not to mention a few of the benefits listed in Psalms 25, 31, 33, and 34: those who fear Him gain instruction, lack nothing, and receive great goodness; His eyes are on them; and encamping angels surround them, bringing deliverance.

Spending time in the psalms also changed my walk with God. By reading of David's "heart after God" through his convictions, intensity, and love for the living God, I was forced to examine my heartfelt feelings toward Him. Could I say, "I love You, Lord," with emotion or with head knowledge alone? I so admired David's total heart after the person and Word of God that I, too, gained a strength and intensity in my relationship with God by rewriting pertinent verses in the psalms until they became my own expressions.

The psalms became two-way conversations. I rewrote five to seven psalms, choosing the words and verses that genuinely described my particular, current circumstances or emotions, and God began to speak to me through concurrent verses. Almost as if I felt His touch or heard a voice, I began to recognize a "word" from the Lord, *just for me.*

One February I was to share my testimony at eight high-school assemblies, five being public high schools. High schoolers would be *required* to attend, but more than likely didn't *want* to hear an adult talk about the dangers of drugs and alcohol or the love of God. Intimidated, I feared that it would be like going in front of one thousand sharks. (When high schoolers don't agree with you, they'll let you know!)

I had just gotten a phone call from the person who was booking me, and she said, "There is one more high school that wants you to speak. Would you come earlier on that morning?" I grimaced and agreed, thinking, *Oh, boy, okay, I'll come, but I gotta be nuts.*

Later that morning, I opened the book of Psalms where I had stopped the day before, Psalm 89:5. As I was reading and rewriting the verses, I wrote, "The heavens praise your wonders, O Lord, your faithfulness too, *in the assembly* . . . !" God knew *exactly* of my upcoming assembly presentations, my concerns, and even my fears!

Every day I waited for God to speak to me through the book of Psalms. Every day. And I came expecting to hear Him. In *my* words, Psalm 5:3 says, "Lord in the morning, I bring my requests to You. And I wait in expectation for Your answer." Why expectation? Because He is faithful to the promises in His Word. It is not wishful thinking or childish dreaming, but a fact about His character. He answers prayer! My personal prayers of praise expressed my feelings, fears, and hopes, and *without fail*, God responded daily by assuring me of *His* faithfulness and sovereignty.

Admit

The ADMIT section was another pleasant and unexpected surprise. What might have been a time of browbeating turned into a planned time of accountability to God for sins of omission *and* commission, then ended in daily renewal.

My first written words of confession each morning were these:

Search me, O God, and know my heart;
   test me and know my anxious thoughts.
See if there is any offensive way in me,
   and lead me in the way everlasting (Ps. 139:23–24).

By the time I finished writing those verses, I instinctively knew what to confess to God as sin in my life. Just professing the words of Psalm 139:23–24 allowed God's Spirit to reveal my shortcomings of the last twenty-four hours. Short accounts with God released fresh forgiveness and regular renewal of spirit.

When I began the discipline of daily confession in writing, I was the mother of a toddler. I rarely showed my anger in public, but when I was at home alone with my son, he got shaken and yelled at loudly. I let him know that he made Mom mad. It seemed every day I had to talk to God about my uncontrollable anger. Unbelievably, I didn't sense God rebuking with words such as, "You are terribly bad and sinful." No, God's Spirit nudged me, saying, "You don't want Jacob to feel toward you as you felt toward your parents, do you?"

I had experienced a "yelling home" as a child and learned those same explosive habits. But now I had a choice to control those emotions. I could change or get professional help. I could choose to shut my mouth, count to ten, back up, or turn around. I could do any of those things if I just would. *I had not made the decision to change*. Out of genuine repentance, I asked God, by the power of the Holy Spirit, to change me. And over time, that part of me became new.

What also surfaced was a very jealous person who envied people prettier, skinnier, or funnier than myself.

I would want to be their friend, but I wouldn't make an effort to befriend them because they were "better."

One particular instance stood out. A dynamic young volunteer worker came to help in our ministry, but she unknowingly threatened me. She would make appointments with kids, and I would become angry with her, haughtily asking, "Why did you do that without my permission?" Though ashamed of myself, I could barely control my jealousy. I was embarrassed to admit it, but the bottom line was this: kids liked her, and I didn't want them to like her more than they liked me.

Eventually, she just "backed off" because I never gave her an opening to use her skills and gifts. When she moved away, without being able to have an effective ministry, my heart was terribly convicted. God showed me that I had squelched the opportunity of having a super addition to our staff because of the sin of jealousy. With true regret and humiliation, I purposed to change and sought counseling to control my inner thought life.

Some mornings, I would struggle longer in this section than in others. The words *integrity* and *holiness* were now a part of my personal agenda, not merely spiritual terms to describe the theologically oriented or seasoned Christian, but words I was longing to see define my character.

God's Spirit began to gently direct me to Scripture or books or conversations that would lead me to desire holiness. The seriousness of it all certainly didn't fit my personality or my previous track record of impulsive-compulsive behavior; therefore, I would leave that section every morning by writing the words in my own paraphrase: "Transform my mind, please, God. Supernaturally fill me with Your Holy Spirit, overflowing. Cleanse me. Renew me. Change me" (Rom. 12:1–2). It was a fact. The undisciplined person I had been all those years was obviously going to need a lot of transformation. Mother Teresa put it this way: "Our progress in holiness depends on God and ourselves. On God's grace and our will to be holy. *We must have a real living determination* to reach holiness" (emphasis added).

In Luis Palau's book, *Heart After God,* he cajoles,

> Nobody gets fat over night. Immorality begins with tiny things. Little things. Yet, if you don't crucify them, if you don't bring them to judgment, if you don't face up to them for what they are—sin—they can destroy you. They can blur your moral judgment at a critical, irreversible junction in your life. No one sees the little flaws. But everyone sees the big collapse.

Determined to be holy, for *God's* sake, and delighting in the freedom from guilt that comes from daily confession of sin, I genuinely looked forward to a time of daily renewal in the ADMIT section of *My Partner.*

Requests

In the REQUESTS section, my faith was both stretched and made solid. In this type of prayer—asking—I discovered many principles that God Himself set forth in His Word.

Initially, I began with a two-page prayer list of people's names and a phrase or two after each name that would specify my request for them, for instance, healings, interviews, tests, and so on. Praying for *others* created a deep concern and genuine interest in their lives.

In addition, on my list were upcoming events, financial situations, ideas needing further direction from God before pursuing, and dreams and plans for the future.

Then the inevitable occurred.

Questions! Was I asking for too much, too often, over too many days? How long was long enough to pray for something? Was it God's will? Who was *I* to pray so boldly? What was taking so long? Didn't God hear me?

The next obvious step was to search the Scriptures, consider my own motives, and find out what other authors had to say about "requesting" prayers.

Through trial and error I learned that prayer was not just receiving yes answers to every prayer. As C. S. Lewis put it, "The essence of request, as distinct from compulsion, is that it may or may not be granted."

Psalm 37:4, "Delight yourself in the LORD and he will give you the desires of your heart," reminded me to ask, because He truly does want to grant the desires of my heart. But that also exposed that inner work must be done first! Was I delighting in Him—spending time with Him—or just selfishly looking for God to make me happy?

James 5:16 in the New Testament, "The effective, fervent prayer of a righteous man avails much" (NKJV), proved to be much like Psalm 84:11, which stated, "No good thing does he withhold from those whose walk is blameless." As I applied those Scriptures to a prayer request list, it was essential to ask two questions during the interim time of waiting upon God's answers:

1. Is this a "no good" thing for which I'm asking? Is it in agreement with God's written Word, in accordance with the law of the land, and in keeping with personal integrity?
2. Has my "walk" been blameless? Am I making right choices, are my words truthful, do I slander others, and do I keep my oaths (as listed in Pss. 15; 24)?

But once again, James 4:2–3 simply kept me asking, challenged me to check my motives, and then cautioned me not to doubt, but trust in God's *best* provision—whether it be yes or no.

What began as a simple prayer request list developed into a fifteen-page, exciting, five-year, faith-filled adventure with God!

Thanks

To close MY PART of prayer each morning, I would handwrite a thank-You note to God. Simply put by O. Hallesby, "To give thanks means to give glory to God with our lives, with the wonderful things that happen and how He works within us."

Acknowledging God's sovereignty and intervention in every single area of our lives—feelings, finances, family, friends, *and* the future—is a daily reminder of our humanness and His divine omniscience. Oh, we can get cynical, grumpy, lazy, or forgetful of all the good that God brings into our daily lives, but THANKS is to remember how often He forgives us and how carefully He delivers us from trouble. A thank-You note ushers arrogance into the sunset and gives God the glory and honor due His name. No more checkoffs on the list of wants, but gratitude for His goodness and grace, expressed in writing by the recipient.

God's Part

Listening

The LISTENING section of *My Partner* proved to stump me initially. It involved some risk. If I listened, would the God of the universe speak to me? I recalled hearing directions for a rookie listener: "Put your pencil to the paper, then ask God, through His Holy Spirit, to speak to you and begin to write."

Still not confident, I found more good books by Andrew Murray, such as *The Prayer Life, Inner Life, Confession, Forgiveness,* and *Christ on the School of Prayer,* that opened my eyes about the inner life, spiritual disciplines, and Murray's actual experiences of listening to God. His books provided information and biblical references, blowing away much of the fogginess attached to listening to God.

As A. W. Tozer explained listening to God in *The Pursuit of God*, it became more tangible:

> I think the average person's progression will be something like this. . . .
> First, a sound as a presence walking in the garden.
> Then a voice, more intelligible but still far from clear.
> Then the happy moment when the Spirit begins to illuminate the Scriptures and that which had only been a sound or at best a voice now becomes an intelligible word, warm and intimate and as clear as the word of a dear friend.

Listening to God was not intended to be magical or mystical or frightening. Our attitude should be to fear God but not what He might say. The greatest problem with listening to God is not obeying what is heard!

One day, I had stepped over the boundary of hearing and not doing. While writing in my LISTENING section, I simply wrote down the phrase, "Watch your driving." That phrase, not being particularly scriptural, caused me to consider it a rather unusual journal entry. Nonetheless, I had a distinct feeling that I would be challenged that day in the area of driving.

One hour later, I was pulled over by a policeman who proceeded to give me a sixty-dollar ticket for speeding! I got out of the car and stood on the side of the road as he finished writing up my ticket. He said, "Lady, get into your car. You're going to get hit!" I was shaking my head and crying in disbelief. I hadn't listened! God had told me to "watch my driving," and I hadn't listened.

Listening to God is for anyone. It is a discipline learned and developed through practice. Some of us have never tried it, while others listen to God regularly. If we would just plan time to listen and have a willing heart, He will meet us there. As Psalm 25:14 promises, "The LORD confides in those who fear him; he makes his covenant known to them."

Messages

The MESSAGES section of *My Partner* is the place to take notes of sermons and Bible studies in order not to miss or forget God's word revealed at any given time. Approaching each convention, sermon, or weekly meeting with an attitude of openness toward change—the good and the bad—allows God's voice to be heard.

Recently our pastor was interviewing a fellow who "pretithed," giving monetary gifts to his church *before* generating the income. I was scribbling down notes of the discussion when I literally looked up and thought, *Hey, I should do this, too!* Knowing our high-school ski camp was the following weekend, I decided to offer one scholarship if someone had the need. Upon leaving the church service, I bumped into the high-school intern and began to mention my desire to offer a ski trip scholarship. Two minutes later, a student joined in step with us. He couldn't afford to go to camp, but was there any other way? You bet!

I know of *three* separate times that my pastor, Dr. Schuller, has preached a sermon that has inspired me to take gigantic steps of faith. The dream to write a book, detailing my life as a teenage alcoholic, became reality after listening to sermon after sermon by Dr. Schuller on believing in God's dreams for one's life. Years later, June 1987, *Just One Victory* rolled off the press! The outline for the prayer notebook, *My Partner*, came after hearing a motivational Sunday morning message. A third sermon caused me to persevere during difficult times, doubling notebook distribution rather than completely stopping production.

I'm thoroughly convinced that God intends to speak through my spiritual leaders, and taking notes won't allow me to miss or forget what is said. Having pen and paper ready during a sermon causes concentration and encourages one to apply what is heard.

Hebrews 13:7 exhorts us to "remember your leaders, who spoke the word of God to you. Consider the outcome of their way of life and imitate their faith." Convention speakers, retreat and conference workshop leaders, spokespersons on Christian radio and television—all provide God's Word to the believer on a continuous basis. The Word of God, spoken through our leaders, has the power to send us out changed from the way we entered!

New Testament and Old Testament

Psalm 130:5 explains the way I've grown to view my Bible reading: "I wait for the LORD, my soul waits, and in His word I do hope" (NKJV).

Both the New Testament and the Old Testament have been constant sources of encouragement, correction, direction, and comfort. I've decided to read through the Bible each year; therefore, I read *The One Year Bible* (Tyndale House), one of many resources available for that purpose.

But *boring, monotonous, exhausting,* and *irrelevant* are not words that describe my planned time in the Word. More descriptive words would be *life-changing, risky, adventurous, faith-stretching, comforting,* and *motivating.* When I was a young Christian, my mentor (and husband) advised me to daily read the Bible and *not put it down* without hearing from God.

How? I let the Word speak to my soul. From David's discourse in Psalm 119, I've learned to allow the Word to

- Keep me from sin (v. 11)
- Open my eyes to new and wonderful things (v. 18)
- Counsel me (v. 24)
- Strengthen me (v. 28)
- Give me understanding (v. 34)

85

- Direct my paths (v. 35)
- Turn my eyes from worthless things (v. 37)
- Be the theme of my song (v. 54)
- Teach me knowledge and good judgment (v. 66)
- Make me wiser than my enemies (v. 98)
- Keep my feet from every evil path (v. 101)

Psalm 19:11 says it concisely: "By them [the commands of the Word] is your servant warned; in keeping them there is great reward."

I've found it essential to have a pen and a highlighter to accompany my Bible so that I can date and underline a Scripture passage of promise, direction, or hope. Seeing dates and references beside Bible verses, in itself, can be a reminder of God's faithfulness. In fact, when tempted to doubt God's timing or to be discouraged, I'll peruse my Bible, just to remind me of His continuous intervention in my life.

One such time was on a ramp of the freeway. On the way to the Christmas Eve service at the Cathedral, my tire popped and flattened—miles from the church. If that wasn't enough, the spare tire was combination locked beneath the rear of the van (and I forgot the combo!). Therefore, no tire, no jack, no fix. Knowing that the gas stations were closed and all help was at church, I decided to go to a phone booth, leave a message so that my husband could find me at the close of the service, and sit tight until help arrived.

With at least an hour to wait, I opened my Bible to the book of Psalms and began to read familiar verses, wondering why I was sitting in a cold van and not a beautifully decorated, warm church! Some twenty minutes later I noticed Psalm 116:7 underlined with a date beside it: "Be at rest once more, O my soul, for the LORD has been good to you."

I smiled, thinking, *Yes, God has been good to me . . .* , and before I could finish the thought, my peripheral vision caught a shiny red one-ton pickup backing up to my vehicle. After I explained my dilemma, the young fellow proceeded to open his back hatch and pull out wire cutters and a hydraulic jack. Within fifteen minutes I was on my way to church!

Had this been the exception in my life, I would have passed it off as coincidence, but God's Word was *continually* causing me to *hope* in Him, then watch Him do incredible things everywhere I turned.

A young friend of mine, Jim Bennett, had a lifelong dream of becoming a big-league baseball player. During his last two years of college baseball, he also volunteered weekly in our high-school ministry. Soon, his dream became ours, too. In his senior year when the spring draft approached, we all prayed with great fervor for God's will in this matter, but God did not allow the door to open at that time. Somewhat disheartened, but still believing in Jim's dream, we continually prayed for an open door for him to enter the major leagues.

Almost two months had passed without a serious call from an interested club, yet we could not give up praying for a miracle. It was even difficult to talk about, almost like asking an overdue pregnant woman if she had had her baby yet, only creating more anxiety when the answer was repeatedly no. Even as close friends began to give up hope, a few of us held on to the only fact left: we believed that God had put this dream in Jim's heart and we had to trust Him, somehow, to bring it to pass. One thing was certain. It would take God's intervention because the draft had been completed over a month earlier.

One July morning, in my quiet time, I read a Scripture verse that brought Jim to mind: "*Do good*, O LORD, to those who are good, to those who are upright in heart" (Ps. 125:4, emphasis added). I wrote Jim's name in my Bible and prayed, "Lord, He's so faithful to You and to the ministry with high schoolers, please . . . please . . ."

Feeling prodded by the Holy Spirit, I decided to

call Jim. I found him home midmorning, probably waiting for a call—but not from me. I said, "Jim, I believe in your dream and that God *is* going to bring it to pass. I know how that waiting feels. I, too, have a dream that seems elusive. But, I got a Scripture this morning. I believe it's for you. Would you like to pray together and ask God to open a door this week?" Jim seemed excited and confident. We shared verses and prayed for each other's long-awaited dreams. That very night Jim Bennett was called—and signed—with the Seattle Mariners!

You just never know what time in the Word will bring. It's too great a risk to miss even one day.

Proverbs

Daily reading in Proverbs—a verse or a chapter— always brings an "elbow's nudge" to a situation. As practical as advice can get for daily Christian living, Proverbs has a timely word for its reader.

For the procrastinator, Proverbs 24:33–34, "A little sleep, a little slumber . . . and poverty will come on you like a bandit," serves as a pointed reminder to get up and get going! Everything from getting wise counsel to guarding what comes from one's mouth (i.e., gossip or nagging) to warning against adultery unfolds throughout the thirty-one chapters (that makes it convenient to read one for each day of the month)—reminding us that the instructions in the book of Proverbs still apply to today's believers.

The book of Proverbs is actually a relevant guide for living the Christian life. Chapter after chapter is filled with simple but solid advice.

Should I follow the crowd?	Read Proverbs 1.
Is morality outdated?	Read Proverbs 2.
How can I be wise?	Read Proverbs 3.
Affairs? Adultery?	Read Proverbs 4–7.

What's better than money?	Read Proverbs 8.
What's wrong with a little "fun"?	Read Proverbs 9–10.
What's the point of being proud?	Read Proverbs 11–12.
A quick temper?	Read Proverbs 13–15.
Plans? Decisions?	Read Proverbs 16.
What is the relationship between pride and the tongue?	Read Proverbs 17–19.
The price of procrastination?	Read Proverbs 20–22.
Taking advice?	Read Proverbs 23–24.
What about honor and integrity?	Read Proverbs 25–27.
Accepting criticism?	Read Proverbs 28–29.
Advice for life?	Read Proverbs 30.
Signs of an exceptional woman?	Read Proverbs 31.

A proverb has a powerful way of influencing your day if you read it!

To Do

Though TO DO was not in the acrostic of MY PART or GOD's PART of *My Partner,* ideas, thoughts, and reminders would pop into my head while praying and reading the Bible. Psalm 90:12, "Teach us to number our days, that we may gain a heart of wisdom" (NKJV), became a daily prayer as time with God continued to reveal just how important each hour of the day *could* be if used wisely for Him. I wanted desperately to be a good steward of my time, but I lacked certain disciplines. The need to organize my time became evident, and a TO DO list for each day was a must!

It has been interesting to watch how prayers turn

into dreams and goals. Continuous prayer about goals becomes the motivation to live out these ideas and turn them into action steps on a TO DO list and calendar. A daily quiet time became the appointment with the General of my life so that I would receive today's—and tomorrow's—"marching orders."

I had been given an idea *in* prayer *for* prayer that had radically changed my entire life. No longer would I consider omitting from any day an appointment with God. I was convinced, along with Peter Marshall, that "when I neglect to pray, mine is the loss."
Written prayer became my focal point.
Recording God's answers,
journalizing my heart's thoughts, and
praying through specific prayer request
lists
became my accountability.
My Partner was the "place" for a daily appointment with God and the organizational tool that made it happen every day—and I eventually made it available for many others to share.

Friends of *My Partner Prayer Notebook*

It was all systems go, and life was moving along like an Indiana Jones adventure—full of excitement, suspense, and the thrills of overcoming the enemy. Soon more and more adults and teens wanted me to share about the power of prayer in my life and the *My Partner* system of writing out conversations with God. Women's ministries, churches, and organizations began to request prayer workshops and seminars, and as a result, I received letters from many people—young and old—who were finding God to be real through their written conversations with Him and were pleased to find an organized tool (similar to their personal calendars) for their daily time with God. But most exciting and touching were letters from those whose lives had truly found release from guilt, courage to change, and renewal in their personal relationship with God. They had stories they wanted to share as a result of their new decisions to write their prayers, and I've included a few of them here.

Birgette wrote from Paradise Valley:

I began a study and prayer time based on your ideas. . . . it's so exciting to see answers to prayer! If I hadn't written down the prayer requests I would not have been able to see God's hand at work! PTL!

Alice wrote from Illinois:

I accepted your challenge to spend at least an hour with the Lord every morning. This has been one of the greatest spiritual weeks of my life. The Lord has awakened me early every morning to keep my appointment with Him. . . . [The *My Partner*] formula for quiet time has helped me organize my devotional time and writing everything down keeps my thoughts on track.

Caryn wrote from Minnesota:

I am in a leadership training program. When I complete the program I will be able to counsel at camp. My instructor was reminding us of the importance of having a vital quiet time—so we could guide students *and* know what we were talking about when we told them about quiet times! At that point I realized that my quiet time was just something that had to be *done* every morning. Through your "program" my quiet time has become exciting.

Rebecca wrote from California:

After spending two years in a diminished relationship with God, I have been asking God to show me a way to get back on course with Him in an intimate, rather than

91

superficial way. I have let my struggling marriage draw me away from God. I believe *My Partner* notebook will truly help me to seek His kingdom (righteousness, peace and joy) once again in my life and cause a spiritual renewal.

Kristin wrote from Colorado:

I was feeling my quiet times were just kind of humdrum—the new notebook has just added a spark. (Plus you know how I like to be organized!) I'm making a new commitment to the Lord to get up earlier and have a "real" quiet time. . . . It's easy to have long quiet times on the weekend and I've found them getting too short during the week.

Janet wrote from California:

At the retreat you shared how you had started spending an hour a day in prayer. For some time and through different people, the Lord had talked to me about that and for short periods of time I would try. But there was never that commitment that endured with the passing of time. The Lord had me at that retreat to hear you share. It was as though this was the time to make a definite commitment and I did.

The idea of writing out my prayers really appealed to me. So often during prayer I would lose my train of thought, forget what I had prayed about or fall asleep. It didn't seem to matter what time it was or where I was or what position I was in. There is something about writing things down that overcomes most of those problems. . . .

Much has happened since I made that commitment. I have found myself in hotel rooms with non-Christian friends and somehow found a way to get my hour in. I have been on vacation and have gone back to work full time. I have had my hour of prayer early in the morning and late at night. Because of working full time, I had to stop teaching a women's Sunday school class and because of that found myself without my group of Christian support. That hour a day spent with the Lord has kept me grounded and focused and I pray on target. I have shared with many friends how blessed I have been writing out my prayers. And I have really come to realize that prayer is a conversation between me and my heavenly Father—time for me to speak to Him and for Him to speak to me through His Word.

Janet continued:

You made the comment that you didn't *tell* God . . . (as in demanding) . . . but you *ask* God for specific requests and that if they are God's will that He let you know. You also said that you ask forgiveness for sins in your daily life.

I have seen God answer prayers in my life in marvelous ways and yet it is so easy to forget or become so involved in daily problems and not look to God to take care of the situations. I think it is wonderful to write down these experiences even if they may seem so small so that if we need to be encouraged we can go back and read. On Thanksgiving Day . . . my husband and I started to write all the answers to prayers or blessings God has shown us. I would recommend the idea to everyone!

It is a simple fact. Some of us sincerely want to take positive steps in our prayer lives, but we need a little nudge—or possibly a tool—to help us remain accountable and organized when our nature or personality leans toward procrastination or disorganization. For those who fall into those categories, *My Partner* is an already organized prayer notebook—a tool for making and keeping appointments with God and for recognizing and recording—in writing—the awesome, incredible, life-changing conversations one can have with the Lord, not to mention the power that is released when one prays!

PART IV

■

Delights, Desires, Dreams

CHAPTER

8

Powerful Prayer Principles

My daily appointments with God were power-releasing, faith-producing times that kept me accountable to God. Each new day was like an adventure awaiting me.

Eventually I became curious about patterns recurring in prayer, so I checked a concordance for the verses in the Bible that contained the words *ask, believe,* and *pray.* What I discovered was an unbelievable power source awaiting the believer. Some of the verses appeared too good to be true, almost challenging one to test their validity.

Having heard some of these verses discounted at previous periods in my Christian walk, I set forth my findings cautiously, though there was nothing cautious about them. Believing them as truth meant risky living—daring faith!

Over time, principles about prayer unfolded by observing Jesus' prayer life, applying His directives about prayer to actual circumstances, and imitating the way the New and Old Testament heroes talked with God. Though not an exhaustive list, six types of prayer became evident. Interwoven with the Word, the following patterns established biblical principles for personal prayer:

- Receiving prayer
- Believing prayer
- Revealing prayer
- Interceding prayer
- Agreeing prayer
- Persevering prayer

Receiving Prayer

Simply, but boldly, James 4:2 states, "You do not have, because you do not ask God." Taken literally, certainly it must mean it is okay to ask God, but James 4:3 adds, "You do not receive, because you ask with wrong motives."

Therefore, a prerequisite of any request must be to *ask* of God. Don't *worry* about, *wish* to the stars for, or *demand* of Him what you want or need. Just ask! Second, examine your motives, the intentions or reasons for which you ask. Inquire of yourself honestly, Is this request simply to spend on my own pleasures? Both verses, if applied to daily life, become reasonable, scriptural guidelines for praying—powerful and effective!

In January 1988, I had to make a business decision about expanding or dissolving my three-year-old small business. I was faced with the challenge of needing $12,000 to move ahead—or requiring no money to give up. Giving up seemed a lot easier, but I truly did not believe it was God's best. Assuming a large loan seemed inappropriate, but it was an option. In a quiet time one morning, I got the idea to negotiate twelve monthly payments of $1,000—which seemed more manageable— yet still a bit unreachable. It was a saying by Dr. Schuller that gave me a push in the right direction: "You don't have a money problem. You have an idea problem."

For two weeks, I prayed daily about where to get the initial capital. I knew (at least firmly hoped) that once I had the merchandise, it would generate the subsequent monthly payments. I just needed that first $1,000. Then I began to worry and fret. If this was God's idea, where was His provision?

As I was driving down my street toward home, the words of James 4:2–3 popped into my head, "You do not have, because you do not ask . . ." Let's see, I've worried and fretted over this, and I don't believe that the capital is for my pleasure, but for getting prayer notebooks into people's hands . . . have I simply asked? After pondering that question, I could not say I had come right out and asked *God* for $1,000.

So, I did. I prayed, "Lord, would You give me $1,000 for the first monthly installment?" As I punched my garage door opener and pulled into the driveway, my husband stuck his head out the door. He said, "Beck, your brother's on the phone." Having *just* prayed that prayer, I whispered to God: "Could this be an opportunity?"

Without delay, and probably little forewarning, I asked my older, single brother if he had $1,000 I could borrow for about one month. Without hesitation he said, "When do you need it?" I answered, "Tomorrow!"

Two weeks later, I paid my brother back in full *with* interest . . . and the rest is history!

Scriptures, including James 1:2–5, convince us that God wants us to *ask* Him about everything and He will not rebuke us for asking. He doesn't always answer yes or in our timing, but the Word clearly encourages believers to ask of God.

In Matthew 7:7–8 Jesus said, "Ask . . . seek . . . knock." He seemed to be saying, "Just don't sit by and expect things to happen. Write a letter, do research, or even go door to door, and doors *will* open!"

A very well-known national author and speaker, Dr. Norman Vincent Peale, was coming to our church. Because of his inspiring life, a little time with him was probably worth a year of motivation for a young author. But how was I to get an appointment with him? I prayed *earnestly* for God to open a door.

Just ask, seek, knock. It doesn't cost anything to ask, and it will hurt only a *little* if he says, "No!" Anyway, not to ask for an appointment produced more anxiety.

At the suggestion of a friend, I dropped off a letter of request for an appointment at Dr. Peale's hotel and was delighted to receive a call scheduling an appointment with both Dr. *and* Mrs. Peale!

The fifteen-minute appointment turned into an hour and a half of ideas, encouragement, inspiration, and prayer. Near the end of our time together, I asked Dr. Peale for ideas on promoting personal prayer. He suggested that I write an article and submit it to a Christian magazine. He reminded me that people weren't going to always ask of me, especially if they didn't know me or hadn't heard of me.

Upon returning home, I immediately sent a query letter to an editor of a specialized Christian magazine, and believe it or not, I received an acceptance of a reprint of my first article on prayer. I thought, *Hey, this principle is dynamic!*

Receiving so many answers from God created a barrage of questions about prayer. Many people believe that asking God about large-scale needs is okay, but insignificant requests are only a bother to Him. Searching the Word once again convinced me that He wants us to consult Him about everything. Who better is there to consult or discuss options with than God?

Philippians 4:6 seemed direct encouragement to a pray-er: "Don't worry about anything; instead, pray about everything" (TLB). The prayer premise became (1) if God had exceptions, He would have listed them and (2) He wouldn't have used the word *everything* if He hadn't meant everything. Therefore, to pray about everything should affect

- Personality struggles
- Trials
- Finances
- Family relationships
- Goals and dreams
- Cars
- Friendships
- Homes
- Vacations
- Lost Christmas cards and contacts
- Emotional hurts

The list goes on . . . and on . . . and on . . . and so does God's intervention.

In Philippians 4:6, the directive to pray about everything is preceded by, "Don't worry about anything." Just as in Matthew 6, Jesus had a better way for dealing with the realities of daily life: "Do not worry about your life. . . . Who of you by worrying can add a single hour to his life?" What was His advice in replacement of worry? "Seek first his kingdom and his righteousness, and all these things will be given to you as well. Therefore *do not worry* about tomorrow" (vv. 25, 27, 33–34, emphasis added).

The song of the year in 1988 ironically projects comical relief with its jazzy chorus, "Don't worry. . . . Be happy." But how can this be achieved on a practical basis in a believer's life?

I attempted to live the "do not be anxious about anything" theory while participating in a large youth convention. Every assignment given to me and every circumstance of the coming week created high levels of stress and anxiety *before* I had even stepped off the plane! I knew I needed a strategy for Spirit-filled convention living. I hadn't even unpacked when out of mental exhaustion I dropped to my knees beside the bed and cried, "O God, help me!" His presence was comforting; His thoughts came over me, "Get down to basics. Remember Philippians 4:6. Don't worry. Pray."

At that point, I made a conscious decision that whenever I experienced that overwhelmed, dull feeling in my stomach or felt bombarded with too many stress-producing thoughts, I would simply pray. I'd admit my anxieties, relinquish my worries, and request His provisions for escape . . . in big or small situations *that* would be my practice.

Within the first hour at my post, I recognized jealous and inadequate feelings bombarding my mind. I stopped them by praying for forgiveness (if I had dwelled on any of them) and requesting God's help in averting them. That lasted two minutes; they returned. I prayed again, vowing that I was not going to be anxious. They returned again; only it was ten minutes later this time. I repeated the pattern until I had totally forgotten there had ever been an original anxiety attacking my thoughts. Only later in bed that night did I even recall the situation.

Encouraged by my initial victory, and determined to go through each day without worrying, I found I constantly had to whisper Philippians 4:6 under my breath as a reminder of my goal. Frantically looking for people seemed fruitless on the large campus, but praying that I would find them brought them around the corner every time. Conversations seemed awkward to initiate, but when I prayed about that, the problem was resolved through seemingly coincidental remarks.

God was proving to me that a willingness to pray, rather than worry, unleashed His power to work and my trust in Him to increase. It became evident that He was willing to bring His peace and patience into the minute or grand daily responsibilities and relationships if I would just not worry and instead pray!

However, when a door does not open as hoped or prayed for, it is essential to believe, even amidst the disappointment or pain, that it must not have been God's best. God's Word, in Matthew 7:9–11, reminds us that God gives "good gifts to those who ask him." As evidenced in Joseph's life and demonstrated in so many Christian biographies, *without fail*, though days, months, or years will pass, God turns to good what seemed a loss or something meant for evil, and He opens a different, *better* door for *all* involved!

Believing Prayer

If the Scriptures weren't convincing enough in stating, "If you believe, you will receive whatever you ask for in prayer" (Matt. 21:22), George Mueller fueled my fire to pray, *believing*. A story about his prayer life became a constant reminder that it is not the impossible, the possibility, or the promise we are to believe in. We are to put our belief in the Promiser—in *God's* power, love, and faithfulness.

Norman Harrison in *His in a Life of Prayer* tells how Charles Inglis, while making the voyage to America a number of years ago, learned from the devout and godly captain of an experience which he had had but recently with George Mueller of Bristol. It seems that they had encountered a very dense fog. Because of it the captain had remained on the bridge continuously for 24 hours when Mr. Mueller came to him and said, "Captain I have come to tell you that I must be in Quebec on Saturday afternoon." When he was informed that it was impossible, he replied, "Very well, if the ship cannot take me, God will find some other way. I've never broken an engagement for 57 years. Let us go down to the chart room and pray." The Captain continued the story thus. "I looked at that man of God and thought to myself, 'what lunatic asylum could that man have come from?' I never heard such a thing as this. 'Mr. Mueller,' I said, 'do you not know how dense the fog is?' 'No,' he replied, 'my eye is not on the density of the fog but on the Living God who controls every circumstance of my life.' He knelt down and prayed a simple prayer and when he finished I was going to pray but he put his hand on my shoulder and told me not to pray. 'Firstly,' he said, 'because you do not believe God will. And secondly, I believe God has. There is no need whatever for you to pray about it.' I looked at him and George Mueller said, 'Captain, I have known my Lord for 57 years and there has never been a single day that I have failed to get an audience with the King. Get up and open the door and you will find that the fog has gone.' I got up and indeed the fog was gone. George Mueller was in Quebec Saturday afternoon for his engagement. I learned from that man that if you know God and if you know His will for your life and circumstances seem impossible, pray believing that God will—and He will!"

I remembered that story when I was stranded in a California airport, unable to get to Tempe, Arizona, to lead a prayer workshop that noon. Upon hearing that the airport was shutting down for at least two hours, I panicked and called the party awaiting my arrival at the other end. The thought occurred to me that George Mueller had faith to believe God would get him to his speaking destination, but I shrugged off the audacity of that thought with the knowledge that I was no "George Mueller."

Our connection was fuzzy as I tried to relay to the person who answered the phone that it looked like it would be over two hours before I'd be arriving at their airport, since some type of construction work had bottled up the runway. I suggested we pray, but reception between us was getting worse. I could barely hear her, but I knew she was praying for God's intervention. Thinking I had said, "Obstruction," she prayed that God would remove the obstruction from the runway so that we could indeed meet on time for the prayer workshop. Hearing, "Amen," I told her I'd call when I had any news and hung up.

I picked up my pieces of luggage, slung them over my shoulders, and maneuvered my way back through the metal detectors to wait for any breaking news. No sooner had I gotten through the line and unloaded all my luggage than a flight attendant came whizzing by me, commenting to a partner that the airport had re-opened. Disbelieving, I found an airport official to confirm the report and jockeyed my way back to the phone. Frantically searching for the phone number I had tucked away, I redialed and exclaimed the quick answer to prayer—there was no longer a delay.

As our plane was soaring across the state border, I asked the gentleman next to me if he had any insight into why an airport would allow construction during a busy weekday morning.

He responded, "Lady, there was no construction hang-up. There was a bomb on the runway that, for some unknown reason, was removed impulsively by a county sheriff rather than wait for the bomb squad to arrive." My stomach turned!

It proved to be an incredible similarity of stories. At that afternoon's prayer workshop I read George Mueller's account and relayed mine to the women. But even more unbelievable was the woman who had prayed for the "obstruction" to be removed, when I had told her it was a "construction" problem on the runway!

The "believing prayer" principle and George Mueller's model of prayer caused me to constantly look for God to do the impossible, extraordinary, and unbelievable in my life. I likened my enthusiasm for prayer and the dynamics it created to the early Christians in the book of Acts—something always ready to explode, erupt, or unloosen. Life with prayer was incredibly exciting and stretching in comparison to life without prayer.

The anticipation in the words of Habakkuk 1:5, "I am going to do something in your days that you would not believe, even if you were told," caused me to hold on to that Scripture, over and over, until I memorized it and made it a part of my daily thoughts. It created an awareness to believe that God had plans in store for our lives that we couldn't even believe.

Being a dreamer, I always seemed to imagine grander scenarios of what God wanted to do with our church, our city, and our ministry. Little would I understand the fullness of this Scripture until September of 1985 when my husband submitted his resignation to the local board of Youth For Christ, giving nine months' notice in which to find and train a replacement for his position as executive director.

A little apprehensive because we did not have our "marching orders" from the Lord for where we were to go next, we prayed diligently that God would show us. Secretly I was praying for the "big one"—an exciting opportunity somewhere special! I took hold of Habakkuk 1:5 and told my closest friends that I believed God was going to do something we would not even believe—something *so* exciting that in our own imaginations we couldn't even devise it!

Things got a bit unnerving when my husband's replacement was chosen in February, and we still had no "call." Then, as circumstances unfolded, on one weekend we were offered two jobs, one in Florida with Youth for Christ and one in California at the Crystal Cathedral.

Because we wanted *God's* will for our lives, it was, in fact, the verse in Habakkuk that showed us which way to go. In all the options of where we could move, and the possible combinations of what we could do as a ministry team, our wildest imaginations had never thought of working together in a large California church—the Crystal Cathedral—even though we had visited and loved California (especially being from Cleveland, Ohio) and had been regular "Hour of Power" supporters. God had done "exceedingly abundantly above all that we [could] ask or think" (Eph. 3:20, NKJV). That's how we knew it was the job for us!

106

Believing prayer has many facets to it. It has received unfair billing by some people as "prosperity blessing" teaching. But when applied biblically, it is the foundation of faith: *"Without faith* it is *impossible* to please God, because anyone who comes to him *must believe* that he exists and that he rewards *those who earnestly seek him"* (Heb. 11:6, emphasis added).

Oh, to believe God for the impossible in our lives—not because we deserve it but because of His awesome love—and to allow Him to be glorified in the results is an extremely challenging but powerful prayer principle for those who believe!

Revealing Prayer

James 1:2–6 says, "Don't be afraid to ask of God. He will not scold you if you don't know. . . . but don't doubt His will, once He reveals it to you" (author's paraphrase).

This Scripture was a helpful principle used for determining God's will for *any* given situation. Having a "feeling" about a request, one way or another, but not sensing God's affirmation or confirmation through Scripture and His Spirit, prompted simple questions, "What *is* Your will, God? How would *You* have me to pray?"

The principle? Rather than try to convince God of something, ask Him to convince you of His will. Once feeling His assurance, through (1) Scripture, (2) His Spirit and yours agreeing, and (3) the godly counsel of other Christians, you're encouraged to wait until He brings the blessing of His answer. Having no time limits, this principle can become a month- to a year-long process in the case of certain requests.

Such was a time in May of 1985 when I attended C.L.A.S.S. (Christian Leaders and Speakers Seminars) not far from home in Columbus, Ohio. C.L.A.S.S. presented methods for speaking the message of a testimony in an organized and dynamic way. I felt as if this was the threshold of something exciting, and my heart burned with desire to go to the ADVANCED C.L.A.S.S. where attendees would be taught advanced technique in public speaking. One problem. It was in southern California, and that meant I had to get by Roger, my husband, and our checkbook. Being on a parachurch ministry staff, we didn't have a monthly income that provided for gallivanting across the country, especially without advance notice or planning.

Nonetheless, I felt convinced that God wanted me to go. But Roger said, "Becky, I give an inch and you take a mile."

"But, Rog, I believe God wants me to go!" I prayed continuously about it, my yearnings only growing deeper. Then one night in bed, I asked Roger to reconsider. I said, "Dear, what would it take for you to believe God wants me to go to ADVANCED C.L.A.S.S.?" Without much delay, Roger replied, "He'd have to pay your way."

Roger didn't make things really easy for me. But I continued to pray fervently and read verses that encouraged me rather than discouraged my requests to God to allow me to go to California *and* to pay my way!

While sitting outside on the thirteenth day, having my quiet time, I had the distinct thought, *Today is the day you'll know!* I actually looked up into the sky and said aloud, "Did You say that, or did I say that?" Matter-of-factly, I decided God must be telling me "today" He would show us His will. I looked for His answer everywhere—in both my mailboxes and in every phone call. By eight o'clock that evening I walked past the telephone and whispered, "Okay. I thought I'd know today. Did I listen wrong? Did You tell me I'd know today, or was I hearing things?"

At 8:30, the phone rang. It was Fred Littauer, calling from C.L.A.S.S. in southern California. He said we'd not met but he had a note that I was interested in AD-VANCED C.L.A.S.S. How could he help?

Little did he know I needed a lot of help—to the tune of about five hundred dollars. Without letting him know my dilemma, I asked about any payment plans or options for attending the seminar. He suggested using a credit card or prepaying in full. Well, that kind of closed the case, but we continued to chat regarding current speaking and writing opportunities. As I hung up the phone, I thought to myself, *Well, I guess I did find out today!*

Ten minutes later the telephone rang. "Becky, this is Fred Littauer again. God has impressed upon my heart to offer you a scholarship to ADVANCED C.L.A.S.S. in June!"

Much later I found out there had never been such an offer before or since that date in time. Boy, was there hootin' in the Tirabassi home that night!

In addition, because of the initial contacts made with a woman at ADVANCED C.L.A.S.S. (later to become a dear friend), my husband and I heard of a job opening at her church, the Crystal Cathedral, and one year later we were hired to direct the youth ministry there.

It has become my practice, without fear of being laughed at or scolded by God, to *ask* Him how I should pray when I am unsure of His will. When He, in His many intricate and intimate ways, reveals His will, the prayer principle is to purpose to pray *without doubting*, no matter how long it takes, until receipt of His promise.

God says to "call to Me, and I will answer you, and show you great and mighty things, which you do not know" (Jer. 33:3, NKJV). Almost to say, "Just ask. It's no secret."

Interceding Prayer

Much of the request section of a prayer notebook is a prayer list: specific prayers for the needs and desires of family, friends, coworkers, Christian organizations, and those we may not even know.

In praying for others, we receive a model for intercession from both Jesus and Paul. Jesus Himself prayed often for His disciples, and Paul verbalized in the beginning of many of the New Testament letters not only *that* he prayed for the saints, but *how* he prayed for them.

In Philippians 1, Paul says that
- He thanks God for the believers (v. 3).
- He feels joy because of their partnership in the gospel (v. 4).
- He prays that their knowledge of God will grow deeper, so they will grow blameless until the day of Christ (v. 9).

Paul also lists in detail how he prays for the believers, saying that he has not ceased praying for them and asking God that they be filled with the knowledge of God's will, live a life worthy of the Lord, and bear fruit (Col. 1:9–12).

Making it a practice to pray for *every* single family member by name each day, lifting up to God (as Paul suggests) their spiritual needs as well as their personal needs, large or small, is simply intercessory prayer.

One particularly small request that I prayed daily was for my son. For the first time I could remember, my nine-year-old, Jacob, had a falling out with a friend. Neither of us could understand the situation, and though we tried, there never was complete reconciliation. Trying to trust God when the friendship did not rekindle, I asked Him if He would bring another friend along for Jacob. I guess the mother's heart hurt more than her son's, for he seemed to handle the indifference—and rejection—much better than Mom did! In addition, I prayed for Jake's personality to become more godly, knowing it takes two to create a solid relationship.

Almost eight weeks later, a little boy, whom he had known for the whole sports season, "all of a sudden" became his best little buddy. To top it off, both dads loved to fish and planned to take the boys out on the ocean. God had given both Jake and his daddy new friends. And as if God wanted the last word, to quiet a mother's heart, Jacob's report card came home that semester with the comment, "Jacob is a well-liked student and has a super personality!"

Another small incident was in relationship to my parents. After being married forty-five years, couples can grow apart in interests. Hoping that my parents could enjoy their later years in life, I began to pray for my mom and dad's friendship. Just about three months later, my brother called. In the course of our conversation, Rick mentioned that Mom and Dad went out to breakfast almost every morning on their way to work. With an inner smile, I felt indirectly responsible for their "breakfast dates," especially since in all our growing-up years it was a *rare* occasion to eat out.

It's really interesting to pray for something to happen in the life of someone else and then watch it happen.

One friend had a definite response whenever I'd ask her to pray aloud—"no!" I asked her for two years, almost every time we ate lunch together, if she would like to say the prayer. She hadn't prayed aloud since she was a child, she related. Then I put that special request under her name on my list. One month later, in my home, I asked her if she would like to pray aloud with me. Hesitantly, she did, and it was a beautiful start to a regular time in prayer together.

On my personal prayer request list, I've added prayers for healing. Many of the people I meet and minister to have drug and/or alcohol addictions. Saying a daily prayer that God keeps them from temptation and strengthens them, removing their desire for the drugs or alcohol, is a tangible way to be involved in their recovery. If we believe that prayer makes a difference in the lives of others, it is essential to make the time on a daily basis to lift others to God.

One such time, a former Campus Life student of mine called our home. Though we hadn't seen him since he had become a Christian in high school, we had heard that his college activities were far from those a Christian should pursue. Daily prayers were said for him *(for years)* to come back to the Lord. In his senior year, Jeff called one night to tell us that a fraternity brother, after a year of working on him, had led him in a recommitment of his life to Christ. As the saying goes, "the hound of heaven" reached him, and since his initial telephone call, letters have arrived detailing his desire to go into full-time ministry!

Healing prayers include family and friends who have had cancer and other illnesses. The commitment to pray daily and specifically for people with tumors can be a true source of hope and encouragement for them. Often, but not always, amazing results to prayer occur.

When told of a friend's recently discovered cancer, we prayed that God would *reduce* the tumor. Many people were praying for her and believing with her for God's healing. We hadn't talked for almost three months when I saw her at a women's meeting. Though cancer is awkward to talk about, I wanted her to know I was praying for her, so I told her I was daily asking God to shrink her tumor. She looked at me, and with a smile, she related that her doctor had recently told her the tumor had shrunk over 50 percent!

Not every person is physically healed, but as Jesus healed when He walked on earth, as many accounts in the Gospels detail, many testimonies conclude that He heals today! Certain aspects of these healings remain somewhat of a mystery for the Christian church. Yet even though we don't understand all about healing, praying for God's healing when someone requires it does not appear to be outside His will or to violate scriptural teachings. Therefore, the principle is to ask Him how to pray, then pray fervently in that way and trust *Him* for the results.

Interceding becomes an action of faith that any believer can perform for any person anywhere in the world. It just takes a commitment of time. Paul urges, "Devote yourselves to prayer" (Col. 4:2), and he points to Epaphras's example to wrestle in prayer for others, to "stand firm in all the will of God, mature and fully assured" (Col. 4:12).

Agreeing Prayer

My dear prayer partner, Kinney, was unable for many years to have children. Those who can bear children usually don't fully understand the emotional pain involved in being barren. But no matter the situation, friends can share the anguish of others in their disappointments and hurts.

In October 1985, Kinney and I attended a women's retreat together, and it seemed a timely lift to her spirits because a recent adoption attempt had failed very late in the procedure, causing her to despair. Not having a lot of answers, we decided to visit the prayer room.

If Kinney and I had been close friends one year earlier, we probably wouldn't have felt that strongly about the power of prayer. But for the previous eight months, we had been on a wild jungle safari, uncovering new truths about prayer as two young thirty-year-olds finally getting serious about the serious things of God.

As we walked into the empty room I mused that this was a first-ever visit to a prayer room in my *entire* life. Compelled to kneel by two chairs, we prayed for almost forty-five minutes over the situation at hand: the inability to have children (though every conceivable test and operation had been tried), a terribly disappointing, incomplete adoption, and now, perhaps even worse, a loss of hope. We prayed. We cried and tremblingly asked God for a baby, allowing Matthew 18:19 to serve as a reminder "that if two of you agree on earth concerning anything that they ask, it will be done for them by My Father in heaven" (NKJV).

That night, during the Hawaiians' concert, a woman neither of us knew tapped Kinney on the shoulder and said, "I understand you are looking for a baby." We slowly looked at each other in both awe and amazement! The incredible account of the next six weeks included an interview, more prayer, lots of applications, renewed hope, and a beautiful baby girl named Ginny! The story of Kinney's Ginny is perhaps the most dramatic account of agreeing prayer that has occurred in my life, but on a weekly basis it has become a practice to sit with family, friends, and staff members at spontaneous and planned moments and lift great and small needs up to God, agreeing upon them in Jesus' name and leaving the incredible results up to Him.

On many occasions, urgent requests will cause praying over the phone with a prayer partner. Because time and miles don't allow us to be together, we'll pray believing that our pressing needs will be heard by God. How exciting to call back after God responds to agreeing prayer and shout, "You *won't* believe it!"

Not long ago I hadn't heard from a person for over one month regarding a proposal I had submitted to his company. Praying daily about the response, but hearing nothing from the firm, caused me to doubt the outcome. Not wanting to doubt or inquire of the company but needing some ray of hope to continue praying, I called my prayer friend, Marita, in San Diego and asked, "Will you pray for me and have your dad pray, too, that they would just let me know something by January 10?" "Of course," she replied.

My confidence was strengthened through her quick response to me, and in addition to the Scriptures in my morning devotions (my regular quiet time of writing out my requests and concerns), I had been reading a book called *George Müller of Bristol*, the biography of his life of prayer. When I ran across this poem, my spirit soared:

> I believe God answers prayer,
> Answers always, everywhere;
> I may cast my anxious care,
> Burdens I could never bear,
> On the God who heareth prayer.
> Never need my soul despair
> Since He bids me boldly dare
> To the secret place repair,
> There to prove He answers prayer.

Next to the poem, in ink, I inscribed my prayer request and the date, January 9.

On January 10 the company's secretary called me. With a little twinge of excitement, I asked her if they had heard anything about my proposal. No. In fact, the person who would know was out of the office.

When we hung up, I pondered the thought, *Well, you asked to know something by the tenth and at least you know that you can't know until next week! That's something . . .*

When the phone rang that same afternoon and my friend from the company said, "Hello," I must have sounded confused by saying, "Why did you call?" He replied, "Why not?"

"You're right," I said. "I asked God if He would have you call today! And He did!"

I was able to discuss the proposal and gain enough hope to continue praying for favor with this company . . . and I almost blew the phone off the hook in San Diego when Marita's secretary answered and I screamed, "He called. God had him call!"

Agreeing prayer can become contagious when others around you see God's hand moving in incredible, sometimes seemingly impossible, situations. One such time was when a couple on my volunteer staff, young in age and in spiritual growth, were really moving toward God in a very positive, renewed faith. They were engaged to be married and had been for two years, but their faith was now really a part of their relationship (which had not been the case when they initially planned to be married). Shortly before the wedding they attended a church "College and Career Night" at a park to play volleyball. In the course of the evening the young woman lost her engagement ring somewhere. It was not until she had gotten home late that night that she realized it was even missing.

Frantic and concerned about the ring because of its sentimental value, she called her fiancé, and they searched everywhere . . . the cars, all the rooms she might have entered. But neither came up with the ring. That left only one place to look—the public park. They prayed fervently and asked God to help them find the ring.

The next morning they got up at five o'clock and went to the park before going to work. Not even knowing where to begin, they walked over to the volleyball court where the bride-to-be had been standing the previous evening. Looking down on the court, they saw a shiny gem. They had immediately found her engagement ring! The fact that they had prayed together and God had answered them so quickly in a seemingly impossible situation brought to their relationship a new ability to trust God to answer prayer. Though the situation at first seemed negative, through it they truly sensed God's intimate love and His rescue just for them.

From large to small agreeing prayers, God continually shows us that He is listening and faithful and that the size of the request is insignificant. For example, on

116

the morning of the Crystal Cathedral Women's Ministry Easter Breakfast, my husband prayed very specifically for me regarding the morning because I was one of the keynote speakers. When I returned home early that afternoon, my husband asked me how the morning had gone. I related a wonderful story of new relationships and new faces at the breakfast. As I shared every detail, his smile grew bigger and bigger. He said, "I prayed for every one of those things to happen in your life today." Not only did I experience God's faithfulness in that situation, but my heart was really warmed to think that my husband agreed with me in prayer over what may seem insignificant to others but was important to me that day.

Praying *with others* for God's intervention in any given situation creates excitement and incentive to keep agreeing in prayer! Lost wallets, potential job opportunities, hopeful marriage partners, finances, the mending of relationships, from details to dreams—agreeing prayer is a faith-building experience, not to be neglected or considered as powerless.

Persevering Prayer

Though long gone to be with the Lord, Andrew Murray has become much like a prayer mentor to many people. In the early 1900s, as a minister in South Africa, he attended a conference that was to change the progression of his life with the Lord. The written stories of the revival that took place in Andrew Murray's heart regarding the "sin of prayerlessness" in his life read like a map, charting a course from self-examination and renewal to a deep dedication to daily appointments with God for any who would follow. As I uncovered more and more of his writing, I would find his books on prayer up to 75 percent off at bookstores, illuminating the fact that the 1980s Christian was not really "into" prayer. Andrew Murray had written volumes on the power of prayer, but they were tucked away and shelved. By reading and rereading certain chapters, one could gain a strength of vision for the power released by prayer. One such principle he would expound upon regularly was to pray and *persevere.*

He said the secret of perseverance was "patience and faith, waiting and hasting." Murray exhorted one to believe that oft-repeated prayer was not wrong or unscriptural. In Luke 18:1–8, Jesus told a parable to His disciples "to show them that they should always pray and not give up." The parable detailed a woman pleading before a judge for justice and mercy. He compared that story to God's children pleading to Him for justice, and He assured the disciples that God's response would be even more merciful. In fact, in another conversation with the disciples on the subject of how to pray, Jesus related a story of a man who received an answer to his requests *because* of boldness and persistence.

There was once a young boy born in 1805 who had lived as a thief, a drunkard, and a liar. He was considered wicked beyond belief. Yet in his manhood he became admired as a beloved family man and respected pillar of the Christian community in England. He was said to have a motto for his life: prayer was the cornerstone with which his life's work was built. He had complete dependence on God and utter belief in the Bible. His work among the orphaned poor was divinely ordained. He prayed for direct divine guidance in every crisis, great or small, and the thread woven through his life was prevailing prayer. He undertook the building of orphanages strictly by means of faith. He never asked for money of people—only of God. He found that any and all the needs of the work were always given and never once came too late. He found that even delay in answered prayer served a purpose. It was said that over one million pounds were received during the years in which the evangelist George Mueller built orphanages and maintained the care of hundreds of orphans. He stressed the importance in ascertaining the will of God before undertaking anything, but he said, "If our trust in the Lord is real, help will surely come." He received thousands of answers to prayer, though for some he waited up to twenty-nine years for an answer.

His example of the principle of persevering prayer saw me through a delicate and difficult matter. Unusual circumstances allowed me to say nothing and to be the recipient of little help, causing intense feelings of anguish and helplessness.

Every single day I would pray and ask God for relief from the seemingly unjust situation. And when there was no outside answer, a search of Scriptures would be the reminder that "God knows," developing a deeper hope in Him and His deliverance than I had the day before.

Exactly three years later, to the day, the issue was completely removed from my life, as abruptly as it had entered, without injury to me or my family. As I look back over the days of doubt and fear, overcome by Word and persevering prayer, it is fair to acknowledge that one's faith is greatly challenged to grow during trials. Prayer then becomes the avenue of daily releasing the anxieties of humanly irreversible situations to God and sensing His presence amidst the unknown. That is when the words of Hebrews 11:1 are able to take form in a believer's life; no longer vague words of theology, they are one's stronghold to pray when weak: "Now faith is being sure of what we hope for and certain of what we do not see."

The principle of persevering prayer became the foundation of many mounds of miracles yet to come.

CHAPTER

9

Mounds of Miracles

The sheer thrill of moving from the midwestern cloudy days, flat terrain, and cold, cold winters to the year-round sunny, warm days of southern California seemed too good to be true! But when reality struck, six weeks was an unbelievably short period of time to sell the house and cars, tie up loose ends, and get in as much time with family and friends as possible—not to mention taking forty-eight high schoolers on a "Florida Breakaway" in the midst of it all.

Perhaps all those reasons prodded me to ask the Lord for something special. It took us two of the six available weeks just to get our house marketable—painting and even putting up new drapes—so when it came to actually listing and selling our home, acquiring a realtor *seemed* out of the question, unless someone was to stay behind or leave an outsider with the burden of selling an empty house and taking care of all the many details of a house sale. So I simply asked, "Lord, would You sell our house in a day?"

I had been reading in Isaiah during the months prior to the big turn of events in our lives, and the chapters were full of promises and promptings to dream and soar and "not be afraid." They were words to put hope in while still waiting for God's plan to unfold.

Chapters 40—60 of Isaiah were marked and dated constantly with comments relating to evangelism, discipleship, and being a messenger of the gospel. As hope gained a foothold that it was indeed God's will for us to move to California, I felt it was not wrong to at least *ask* for His supernatural intervention.

On a Tuesday, I called the newspaper to put in an ad for a "House for Sale," with all the details. The telephone solicitor asked if we'd be having an open house— a one-day showing. I said, "No." She continued to push me, oddly, until I had narrowed it down to that coming Sunday from 1:00 to 5:00 P.M.—the "norm" she suggested for an open house.

Then I began to ask my friends to pray, "Would you pray with me and ask God to sell my house in a day?" Some jumped on the bandwagon with great anticipation, and others chided me by saying, "Well, you know, Becky, God doesn't always do things like that a second time."

Five years earlier, we had outgrown our little home after the birth of our son. With the same inkling that God was prompting, I felt we should put our first little house up for sale on the Fourth of July (not a real hot day for house sales) with a specific, nonnegotiable selling price and without the assistance of a realtor. I believed God wanted our house up for sale that day! When I suggested we do that, my husband thought I was being a bit impulsive, but, with his permission, that morning I hammered a big FOR SALE sign into our front lawn. Unbelievably we had a buyer for our full asking price that afternoon. Therefore, when a few of my friends didn't seem to believe God would answer that prayer, like George Mueller and the captain, I asked them not to pray at all, because I believed God had been giving me Scriptures and an inner confidence—or faith—to believe that He certainly *could* sell our house in a day if He so desired.

That Sunday morning, I went forward to the altar for prayer after the service, again to solicit prayer for our one-day sale. It seemed ironic that even as the "shepherd" anointed me with oil and proceeded to pray for me, he seemed not to pray believing God would, but only that my faith would continue to be strong!

At 1:00 P.M. many visitors streamed through our doors, but by 3:00 P.M. not *one* person had placed a bid on the house or expressed a serious interest in buying it. At that point, my husband went to the car wash, and my son "bailed" on me and went to Grampa and Grandma's down the street!

Alone in my family room, I looked up at God, then down at my Bible, and sincerely asked, "Did I hear You wrong, or did You tell me that You would sell my house in a day?" Opening to Isaiah, I read, verse after verse, hoping for a glimpse or sign of His word to me. Then Isaiah 51:5 stood out on the page as if it were one-fourth inch higher than all the other verses: "My righteousness draws near speedily, my salvation is on the way." "That's it," I said aloud, closing my Bible. He did tell me. And whoever is going to buy this house is on the way!

The doorbell rang and a prospective couple entered. Before I could even start showing them the house, another couple entered the front door. Fortunately, my husband had returned and was coming in the door behind them.

One hour earlier that couple had been headed south on the highway. Picking up the newspaper, they ran across our open house ad and made an unplanned turnaround. By five o'clock that afternoon the sale by owner papers were signed, and the rest is history!

Almost as soon as the excitement of our Ohio sold-in-one-day house had erupted, the pressure of purchasing a new house in California intensified. We seemed helpless to be able to make arrangements, since the day we would move to California would be our first day of work in one place and the last day of work at another. Timing, as usual, was *tight!*

My anxieties were soaring, having sold the last of our securities—home and cars—without replacements for them when our plane would land on May 15, 1986. Catching myself out of sync with the principles of prayer, I knew to release God's power. I was reminded in Philippians 4:6–7 to pray about *everything* and not worry about *anything!*

Soon, a California realtor began to call with options of houses to rent for temporary relocation, but each time certain details caused me to question his suggestions. I had grown accustomed to desiring God's best in any given situation, and each possibility seemed either too far, too much, or too risky. Some compromise always rose to the surface.

Knowing that my conditions were beginning to wear the realtor down, I finally accepted an offer, so as not to take for granted his kind assistance. But even as I hung up the telephone with him that morning, I reflected to myself and God, "Could this *really* be the best place for us? You have done so many amazing things, Lord, to move us from Ohio to California. Do You desire us to take this high-priced, far-from-the-church home?" A verse popped into my head: "My peace I give to you; not as the world gives . . ." (NKJV). *Of course,* I thought, *I need Your peace.*

Wanting desperately for God to speak to me regarding this situation, not knowing exactly where that verse was found, I sat down at the kitchen table to read my Bible. I began in John, chapter 14, only to read these words: "Do not let your hearts be troubled. Trust in God; trust also in me. In my Father's house are many rooms; if it were not so, I would have told you. *I am going there to prepare a place for you*" (vv. 1–2, emphasis added). I closed my Bible and thought, *He is going* there *to prepare a place for me.*

That very morning the women's Bible study group at the Crystal Cathedral discussed the fact that the youth pastor and his family were in need of temporary housing for the summer—were there any availabilities? A Bible study attendee, Clara Landrus, and her husband trekked to Idaho each summer to help on their son's dairy farm. Hearing the need, she mentioned it to her husband at lunch, and he called our home that very afternoon!

Upon his introducing himself to me and offering his home—free of rent—I exclaimed, "He did it." Jesus had gone before us that day to prepare a place for us. What a wonderful and warm start we had as Californians!

And with that same dogged determination I drove another realtor crazy until there was only one week in which to buy a home, allowing for the appropriate number of days for "closing" and "escrow" before Wil and Clara would arrive home from their summer outing.

Now on our own, my husband noticed a little realtor's office next to a dry cleaner. He wanted to go in; I wanted to cry. Housing in California was incredibly expensive, higher than we had originally thought! Disillusioned with the choices available in comparison to our nice roomy Ohio home, we realized it was going to take twice the money to buy half the home.

Daily, I prayed for a miracle, an open door, the right house for us, to no avail. Almost desperate, Roger convinced me this might be our last hope for a home; otherwise, we would need to move to an apartment and keep looking. I couldn't face another move, so I agreed to talk with another realtor. Even though he was friendly, I was not very responsive to his pitch.

Finally I said, "I've been praying a lot about our

future home," then added we had only so much money and one week left to buy a home. He gave us a rather confident smile, though he knew we were asking for a miracle. He, too, was a Christian; therefore, we closed our discussion with prayer, asking for God's special intervention—to show us the way to go!

Though, secretly he and my husband looked at a few houses that week, the first house he showed me that next Saturday became our little home, with all the desires of my heart included! *And,* appropriately, the move-in date was two days before the Landruses were to arrive home. The selling realtor found these coincidences beyond explanation and, thinking I had connections with Dr. Schuller, said, "Hey, you must have had help from the big guy." I laughed, "Our help came from the Bigger Guy!" He laughed, too. The timing, once again, stretched us to persevere in prayer for God's best, reminding us of His perfect, intimate plan for our daily lives (Heb. 10:35–36).

Daily prayer became the opportunity to communicate to God our needs, hopes, and desires, asking for His best, and waiting and watching for His will to unfold—always beyond our expectations and always in *His* time frame. Oh, how perseverance develops faith!

In addition to each miracle that would cause me to hope in God whenever discouraged or impatient, the book of Psalms became my pattern for waiting upon Him. No matter the request—personal, emotional, financial, or relational—I learned to ask Him for daily deliverance and trust in Him *because* of His previously proven character. Verse after verse reminded me to "appeal [to] the years of the right hand of the Most High . . . [to] remember the deeds of the LORD . . . and [His] miracles of long ago . . . [to] meditate on all [His] works and consider all [His] mighty deeds."

CHAPTER

10

Open Doors, Onward Dreams

I was convinced that meeting with God for an hour a day continually provided new ideas, goals, and dreams. As encouraged by Psalm 119, I used the Word of God as my counselor and path lighter and allowed prayer to be my soul's expressions to Him. Receiving an idea from God and then watching it explode into reality was incredibly exciting and encouraging. But hindsight usually was more impressive than trudging through the steps of a dream day by day—especially when others didn't have the same enthusiasm *or* when help was not on the horizon. Perhaps that is just where God would have us, dependent on His deliverance and helpless within our own strength, allowing Him to become strong in our weakness and receive the glory for miraculous answers to prayer.

One such idea that developed into a reality was the original *My Partner,* self-published when my impetuous nature couldn't wait to make available an organized tool for journalizing prayer. I believed that if one had the proof in writing of God's intervention, assistance, and deliverance, that alone might be enough to keep one committed to daily appointments with God. But in the harsh world of business, initiating the publishing, distribution, and sales was not worth anyone's risk, except my own!

After many persevering prayers for God to send help, within a few months into the small business of making, selling, and distributing *My Partner Prayer Notebooks,* a special friend offered capital for increasing the volume of notebooks for availability. In other words, God brought someone else along to believe in and finance the idea God had given.

After two years of prayers, rejections, hard work, a ton of decisions, and knocking on doors, we had sold four thousand notebooks. Later, a publishing house agreed to republish the notebook, alleviating many of the production and distribution responsibilities, and the dream rolled on.

The subject of prayer when discussed as "power waiting to be released" caused men and women of all ages to begin to react as I had. If believers would *only* give God their time and love, fear Him, and believe what He said in His Word about prayer, He would give them the desires of their hearts. Psalm 37:4 declares, "Delight yourself also in the LORD, and He shall give you the desires of your heart" (NKJV). Perhaps the power hidden in that verse is not what are my desires, but how can I delight myself in the Lord?

With the freedom to dream and pray came a release, as if a waterfall had broken through a dam. More dreams and plans, goals and ideas daily unfolded in my hourly appointments with God—and so did corrections, confessions, and creations. The mounds of miracles only fueled more hope to dream God's dreams, and as I approached each day, He seemed to allow big and little doors to open and close along the way, vividly serving as signs of His direction, goodness, faithfulness, and power.

As always, Scripture entwined with prayer increased my faith to hope and dream and watch for God. Over a four-year period, a classic example of a dream implanted in my heart by God was realized.

The same friend who had originally loaned the start-up capital for *My Partner* had attended a large youth congress of the Covenant Church denomination in 1984. Upon returning, he and his sister excitedly shared their experiences of spending a week with four thousand kids and the ways in which God had changed lives. They commented wholeheartedly that a workshop on prayer would have been ideal for a convention such as that! With their encouragement, I decided to daily pray and ask God to open doors for me to attend the *next* CHIC (Covenant High Congress) in four years— 1988.

During this time, unbeknownst to me, my name had been suggested to the speakers search committee, and someone was asked to observe one of my speeches while attending a National Youth Workers Convention in the fall of 1987. Though I knew nothing of these arrangements, I continued daily to ask God for open doors to share about prayer at CHIC '88.

Then in February 1988, I overheard a few of my speaker buddies commenting about a summer congress they would be attending—CHIC '88! Their excitement for the congress—and confirmed speaking dates—startled me into realizing that CHIC '88 was long planned and I was not going to be a part of that particular congress. Disheartened, I almost took CHIC '88 off my prayer list. For some reason I hadn't gotten around to it when I received a message in my office mailbox from a person in Massachusetts I knew I had never met but was from a Covenant Church. As I dialed the phone number, my hand began to shake and my heart leaped with hope that something related to CHIC was developing.

And so it was! Randy, indeed, had called to ask me if I would *consider praying about* being a speaker for

CHIC '88—all the while apologizing for the late notice. I said, "Oh, my goodness, you won't believe this," and I proceeded to tell him of my three-and-a-half-year-long prayer request. Much more than coincidence, God had put a desire in my heart, allowing it to come to pass in such a way as to give Him the glory! Psalm 37:4, "Delight yourself also in the LORD," popped into my heart and mind as reality, not conjecture.

But that was not to end the excitement of a long-awaited answer to prayer. Two years earlier, I had attended a women's conference, and while listening to a keynote speaker, I was struck with the idea of writing a devotional for teenagers.

From that moment on, the idea would not go away, so I added it to my prayer list as a potential project needing God's help. I continued to ask God for His ideas and open doors, and though I gained a few people's interest, the idea seemed to lie dormant, *except* for my daily prayers regarding it.

Two months before CHIC '88, the high-school convention for four thousand students to be held in Colorado, I received a call. "Becky, this is Chuck from CHIC. You may not remember me, but Tic gave me your name. We wondered if you would consider writing a devotional for the high schoolers at CHIC '88 to take home as a follow-up tool? We would need at least four thousand copies." In utter amazement, I told Chuck of my two-year prayer request to write a devotional for high schoolers. He had known nothing of it or of my prayer list!

The topper was an outside underwriter of the total project and the incredible two-month turnaround of a six-week daily devotional called *Live It*.

Prayer had truly become an adventure of faith. Taking Hebrews 11:6 literally, "Without faith it is impossible to please God," propelled me to have faith in God with the fresh abandon of a dependent child. Wanting even more faith, I found Romans 10:17 to be the inter-

PART V

———■———

A Deeper Walk

CHAPTER

11

The Blessings and Benefits of Prayer

Just to pray without ceasing for one hour seemed like a monumental achievement in mastering a difficult spiritual discipline, but my deeper walk with Christ has truly been most meaningful to me. Yes, amazing answers to prayer elicit whoops and hollers and persevering prayer teaches endurance, but spending time with Jesus—perhaps as His disciples did, laughing, crying, complaining, proposing, deliberating, submitting, confessing, and praising—has been the joyful part of our walk together.

Had people told me ten, even five years ago that I would be a prayer motivator, I would not have believed them, nor would my closest friends. I am often prejudged as never serious, perhaps even flighty, until I open my mouth. And of all the suitable topics someone of my personality profile could begin to expound upon, prayer would—without exception—be the last one picked by others as the love of my life.

Perhaps that paradox is the greatest argument I have in my defense when others offer their reasons (or excuses) for not praying. My experience in prayer proves the point that it is not race, sex, denomination,

133

vocation, or education that singles out a person to be an effective pray-er. It is simply one's decision to spend time with the Lord. How one arrives at that decision, whether it is out of crisis, great need, humiliation, or persuasion, seems immaterial. It is a matter of one's time—priorities, personality, and profession all set aside and boiled down to one question: Will I make time for God?

When answered with a resounding, "Yes, no matter what the cost," then the inevitable results of a deeper walk with God occur *because of prayer.*

Prayer allows God's presence into all areas and aspects of one's life, beginning with simple, daily decisions and culminating with one's life's purpose. The combination of prayer and the Word takes conjecture out of life and replaces it with certainties. And in the *practice* of prayer one is escorted farther and deeper into knowing and loving God.

Therefore, imagine one's surprise in stopping after five years of a long journey to look back over the mountains and valleys, to assess progress and be in awe of the unexpected benefits of prayer. The results of diligent prayer appear as illustrious jewels of immeasurable wealth, and just to read a list of them is appealing, but to experience them as personal possessions is life-changing!

On that journey of daily prayer and Bible reading I have experienced *and* benefited in six areas of personal, spiritual growth, not because I am a woman in ministry, but because I am a person intent on spending time alone daily with God.

I discovered that
- Prayer fuels faith to dream and hope and risk.
- Prayer "woos" us to the Word by our *need* to hear God's response to our requests.
- Prayer teaches trust in God through waiting upon *His* timing.

- Prayer reveals God's plan and our purpose in opening up to us detailed directions for both the present and the future.
- Prayer releases God's power to live and walk in the supernatural realm of the Holy Spirit.
- Prayer unleashes love for God—emotional, real, and all-consuming.

Who, then, having thought through the benefits of prayer would consciously decide to eliminate, forget, or neglect time with God? Let's walk on . . .

CHAPTER

12

Prayer Fuels Faith

Now faith is being *sure* of what
we hope for and *certain* of what
we do not see.
　　—Hebrews 11:1, *emphasis added*

How do we receive the peaceful assurance from
God that "all things work together for good to those
who love God, to those who are the called according to
His purpose" (Rom. 8:28, NKJV)? Where does that come
from? How can we be sure we are not just chasing after
an elusive dream, a "pot of gold," or a rainbow? And
where and how does prayer enter into the process of
faith—believing in what we expect to come to pass, but
we cannot visibly see?

With the excitement and anticipation of a new
building project, an architect and a contractor sit with
an owner-buyer, assuring him of successful completion
of the project by displaying blueprints, pictures, and
sketches of similar completed buildings. They show the
owner flowcharts of dates for breaking ground, erect-
ing steel, pouring concrete, and doing finish work, de-

136

tailing all the components of the building, though not even begun, but eventually to be finished and seen by all.

Similarly, time spent with God in conversation regarding dreams and hopes puts a form and plan to one's heart's desires proposing that in God's timing and by His blueprint they *will* come to pass. Daily discussions with God, the Author and Perfecter of our faith, the Architect of our lives, only solidify details, develop a calm assurance, and intensify one's hope for completion of one's "building" providing "brick and mortar" for a previously "vacant lot."

Because an idea or a dream starts in one's heart and mind, faith to believe in it cannot be based on outer circumstances; it must be based on God's inner work of confidence and direction—through His Word and Spirit—which will in turn provide visible "markers" as confirmation along the way.

Yet faith is not passive. It is an action, as is love. *To love* is

> to give,
>> to accept,
>>> to sacrifice,
>>>> to stand with,
>>>>> to believe in.

To have faith is to step in the direction toward what is believed to be the planned course of our lives. It is obeying God in the unseen areas of our lives. And because it is fueled by God alone, faith cannot develop without prayer and the Word. It is the consecutive string of thoughts, Scriptures, and promptings heard in the inner person, "Keep moving . . . turn here . . . stop briefly . . . knock on this door . . . step quickly," that propels us through the course of a dream, a project, or an idea.

But how can we obey if we haven't heard Him speak? Prayer and the Word

whisper,
  call out,
    point,
      promise, and
        goad us in each and every step . . .
If we will only make time to listen.

Faith cannot be mustered up, engineered, or manipulated; it is a response from within us, orchestrated by God. It is a supernatural confidence inspired by a supernatural God.

I often shake my head in awe at the miracle of my conversion to Christ. For six years, from the ages of fifteen to twenty-one, I followed all the "popular" trends: going to wild parties, drinking, dancing, bar hopping, and using drugs. I was caught in a downward spiral—going from a normal, happy, all-American kid to becoming an alcoholic drug addict with suicidal tendencies.

An unusual course of events led me to a small church with one born-again, Spirit-filled janitor on its staff who loved to share the person of Christ with the lost. *Never*, in my wildest thoughts, would I have imagined my life turning 180 degrees one hot, sunny, August California afternoon at the persuasion of this janitor.

How did he convince me to be born again when my boyfriend, lifestyle, and future looked so worldly? He spoke these words: "If anyone is in Christ, he is a new creation; old things have passed away; behold, all things have become new" (2 Cor. 5:17, NKJV). And though this janitor knew of my past and present, he told me that Jesus loved me—just the way I was!

And why by his suggestion and without struggle or reservation on my part would I ask Jesus Christ into my heart? Though I could not see ahead, looking back was so painful that the words he spoke offered me hope for a new life. My previous "religious" experiences were not the basis for that all-encompassing, daring faith. Nor had I been able to quit drinking or drugs out of my own self-determination. No, I was *without hope* for healing, no money for even outpatient recovery. I had literally depleted any reservoir of self-respect. What could cause such a turnaround?

I believe the first step of faith took place when I *believed* what that janitor said about his Jesus: (1) He did and would always love me, and (2) He *was* going to make my life new.

The second step occurred when I repeated the "sinner's prayer," begged Jesus to come into my heart and forgive me of my many sins and make me new. I walked away from that time in prayer convinced I was a brand-new person! There is no other explanation for why the compelling thought or drive to have a drink, that craving or physical need for alcohol, had been removed from my thought life, *never* to return. In that moment of prayer, I was miraculously released from the bondage alcohol had upon me. Equally drastic changes in my lifestyle, friends, and habits were just the initial "wave" of new life in Christ!

Almost immediately strange and "unusual" cravings developed within me, only hours after my conversion:

to read the Bible,
to pray, and
to tell others about Jesus.

To say I was a "sinner" saved would be stating the depth of my depravity mildly. Yet the question remained: How could I have changed so abruptly and dramatically?

I can only attribute the accelerated changes in a few short months . . .

from alcoholic to evangelist,
from "worldly" to spiritual,
from a foul mouth to a clean mouth,
from immoral to moral,

from habitual liar to truth-teller,
from worrier to pray-er,
from pagan to incessant Bible reader . . .
to a *faith* supernaturally implanted within me to *believe* in the living Christ and His Word. The moment I dared to believe that Jesus could and would change my life from old to new, though I could not see how, and chose to believe God's Word as literal, I was rescued, delivered, and saved through faith in the Son of God.

Less than one month after my born-again experience, a small group of Christians laid hands on a completely sober and "straight" twenty-one-year-old and prayed a seemingly unfit prayer. They prayed for God's Holy Spirit to empower me as an evangelist—throughout the world. Strange, huh? I had barely escaped the fires of hell, and they had me gallivanting across the world sharing about Jesus! And it would be months later before I would read 1 Timothy 4:14: "Do not neglect your gift, which was given you through a prophetic message when the body of elders laid their hands on you."

Not knowledgeable regarding Christian organizations or the church, I returned to my parents' hometown and within a year was on staff with a local Youth For Christ chapter. Over the past thirteen years I have been sharing my testimony through both spoken and written mediums throughout the United States and in other countries.

Could I ever have imagined that, in the first months after my conversion to Christ, God would have such a detailed and dynamic plan for one who was *so* lost? No. But faith is believing what you cannot see. It is taking a step toward where you believe God is leading. It is not looking back. It is not trying to rationalize. It is not trying to discover logical reasoning. It is daring to believe that the God of this universe can direct one's life,

able and willing to intervene,
to bring the "dead" spiritually to life,
to bring healing and health,
and to give hope for tomorrow—
no matter now bleak tomorrow looks.

Prayer and faith combine the appointments with the Architect and the subsequent action steps that He directs in fulfilling God's purpose for one's life. Whether it is pouring the concrete of the foundation, laying just one brick in the huge process, or looking back at an addition completed, faith is the "stuff" a Christian's life cannot do without. Hebrews 11:6 challenges, "Without faith it is impossible to please God."

CHAPTER

13

Prayer Woos to the Word

Meant to sustain, inspire, motivate, increase faith, mature, and strengthen a believer, the Word of God, when interwoven with prayer, serves as direction and guidance, conviction and comfort, a deterrent from sin, an escape, a counselor. A deeper walk with Christ is evident when our *first* response, our most compelling desire at any given time, in any situation, is to hunger for the advice found in God's Word.

Theophan, known as the Recluse, said if they were practiced simultaneously, the Word and prayer produced a certain feeling within the believer toward the Lord:

> Do you wish to enter this Paradise as quickly as possible? Here, then, is what you must do. When you pray, do not end your prayer without having aroused in your heart some feeling towards God, whether it be reverence, or devotion, or thanksgiving, or glorification, or humility and contrition, or hope and trust. Also when after prayer you begin to read, do not finish reading without having felt in your heart the truth of what you read. These two feelings—the one inspired by prayer, the other by reading—mutually warm one another; and if you pay attention to yourself, they will keep you under

142

their influence during the whole day. Take pains to practice these two methods exactly and you will see for yourself what will happen.

What *will* happen? "God's spark, the ray of grace will fall at last into your heart. There is no way in which you, yourself, can produce it: it comes forth direct from God."

Recently, on an early evening flight home after an all-day seminar, I sank into my aisle seat, and out of pure exhaustion I stuffed my carry-on bags under the seat in front of me and sighed with relief at the sight of an empty row next to me. Tired, yet keenly aware of the deadline of another project beckoning for my attention, I closed my eyes and wondered if I had enough energy to regear my thoughts. In that brief moment of silence, a thought crossed my mind: *You haven't read your* One Year Bible *yet today.* And the words following that thought were these: *Becky, if you open your Bible, I'll speak to you.* I smiled and sighed with a deep contentment. I prayed, "Oh, You know I need You right now. I'm stretched beyond what I can do. You are here with me, and through Your Word, You *want* to speak to me."

I reached down and pulled out my Bible, *expecting* to hear from my Lord. What I got was more than I had anticipated. While reading in the book of Joshua, I ran across these words: "Choose for yourselves this day whom you will serve. . . . as for me and my household, we will serve the LORD" (24:15).

I closed my eyes, just to reflect on the timing of God's Word—here on a plane, after a long day of coleading a Resource Seminar for Youth Workers, in my heart I felt the Lord's acknowledgment of my service. Ironically, I had been listening to a Praise Strings tape, and the song "Angels Watching Over Me" began to play. I laughed, thinking: *Here I am, up in the air, with the angels, having just served God, praying for encourage-*

ment and motivation, and this tape and those words are falling together at this time.

Then, the plane tipped just a bit, and a warm, bright ray of sunshine filled my empty row and rested on my face. I kept my eyes closed, wanting to soak in as much of God as I could in this moment. The light turned from bright yellow to orange and then to a deep red as I kept my eyes closed. Quietly, I felt I heard God's voice whisper, "Hi!" His voice seemed so casual, so relaxed. So I responded in my thoughts with, *Hi!* I couldn't help smiling. I knew at that point I could let myself discount this encounter or I could just let it flow. I decided to "go for it." The next words I heard were, "I love you." Without skipping a beat, I said, *I love You, too.* Then I felt as if God said, "I know." Tears warmed my cheeks. Our conversation continued for a few minutes. Then as the warmth of the sun withdrew, I looked down at my Bible resting upon my lap. What if I hadn't opened my Bible?

Prayer draws us to the Word, and the two ignite to create a spark, even a flame, for the Lord. The Word and prayer, if *applied* to all circumstances of our lives, are *intended* to change, transform, motivate, and propel us to make certain decisions, take deliberate steps, and stretch to live and walk in the Spirit. But until Bible reading and prayer become our *natural* reaction when faced with a dilemma or a decision, we'll not experience the warmth described by Theophan—the spark that allows God to confirm direction or grant peace amidst turmoil. If prayer is simply a last resort "call for help" and if one only haphazardly searches the Scriptures for guidance (when all other avenues have failed), one has missed God's true intent of how prayer and the Word are able to integrate moment by moment into a believer's life.

Though I've experienced countless situations where God's Word affected my directions and responses, one such time I'll always remember happened during a women's retreat. A negative and hurtful mis-communication occurred. Because we were all Christians, I optimistically confronted the situation, speaking the truth in love, but was thoroughly heart-broken over the rejections that followed.

In my hotel room, I prayed, cried, and spoke to my roommate. Frustrated, I opened the Bible, but disap-pointment and anger kept me from finding comfort in the Word. I proceeded to roll over and turn off the light. Sensing my distress, my roommate made a suggestion, but something didn't seem "right." But what *was* right?

It was then that I knew what was left for me to do. This was a very sensitive situation. I had to be still and look to God (not my friends or my feelings) to show me *exactly* what to do. Therefore, I decided to get up early the next morning to have my quiet time, *search* the Word for God's counsel, and fully express myself to Him, confessing any sin and/or anger on my part. Then before confronting the issue any further, I would call my husband (long-distance) and relay the situation, share my findings, and seek any additional counsel, es-pecially because I was so emotional over the whole epi-sode.

Beginning each morning's quiet time in the book of Psalms, I should not have been surprised that the words of the next few chapters were . . .

"deliver me . . .
    rescue me . . .
        be my shield and my refuge . . ."

In searching my heart and motives amidst this awkward situation of broken promises and in light of the morning Scripture passages, I felt God was on my side. I ran to the phone and relayed my dilemma to my husband. I found him compassionate, but received a strong warning from him to handle the issue gently, let-ting God deal with the broken pieces. During the last day of the retreat, when the outer circumstances did not change, I fought to hold on to my personal integrity though I was tempted to be angry. My only consolation was God's word to me of His faithfulness and promised deliverance.

It was at least six months later when the woman from the retreat, forty years older than myself, called unexpectedly one morning. She said, "Becky, I feel God spoke to me this morning and told me to call you and apologize for what happened at the retreat last year." Almost speechless because I never thought I would hear from her again, I quietly acknowledged her apology.

The comfort of God's Word, in the midst of uncontrollable circumstances, brought His strength and promise into my hurting heart during the retreat, as He knew much more time would be needed to reconcile the relationship. The warmth of God's Word and much prayer became my only resources for "pressing on" during those silent months until His work was complete.

A deeper walk with God emerges when the Word is constantly *blended* with prayer in a believer's life. David mentions several times in Psalm 119 that he put his hope in the Word. Because of that exhortation, it has become my practice to hope in the Word by asking God for a scriptural promise to hold on to or to "hope in" when my endurance level is waning or when I have a long wait or big decision to make. It is as if He gives a promise—His promise—to be my *visible* possession while waiting for the invisible to happen. My Bible, especially the books of Isaiah and Psalms, is splashed with underlined verses, highlighted paragraphs, and dated ink marks next to verses that were my hope during a court case, a broken relationship waiting to be mended, timely sermon texts, encouragement when I needed a lift, guidance for purchasing a new car or in accepting an invitation.

Seeing verse 46 of Psalm 119 underlined and dated

3–1–88 will always remind me of God's promise when I really needed Him: "I will speak of your statutes before kings and will not be put to shame." The week before I was to share my testimony (of being a teenage alcoholic) in an Ohio public high school, I was told the principal was unsure that I would be able to handle all the students because I was a woman. That didn't do much for my confidence, so I opened the Word and asked God to speak to me, confirm His call upon my life, assure me that He would be with me—even go ahead of me. That morning's regular reading in the book of Psalms had me in chapter 119 where God was able to say, "You'll not be put to shame." One week before I had to be at that high school, God's words could not have been more timely or comforting!

The verses that are marked in relationship to my personal situations and circumstances provide great hope within me, though for someone else they may have little or different significance. That is why it is so important to develop one's own regular Bible reading plan, *personally* growing familiar with God's Word *as His voice*. Then we can run to His promises with the fresh abandon of children, reaching for our Father's hand to catch us before a fall or just to feel His warm, firm grip when we're insecure or afraid.

Daily Bible reading, *along* with prayer, encourages a two-way conversation with God, allowing the warmth of the right direction to overpower the dullness or confusion that accompanies wrong or incorrect choices.

In *The Inner Life*, Andrew Murray proposes,

Prayer and the Word are inseparably linked together. Power in the use of either depends upon the presence of the other. The Word gives me guidance for prayer, telling me what God will do for me. It shows me the path of prayer, telling me how God would have me come. It gives me the power for prayer, the courage to accept the assurance that I will be heard. And it brings me the answer to

CHAPTER

14

Prayer Teaches Trust in God's Timing

Suppose a man made me a hundred promises. And he had ten years to fulfill them. In the next month the ten years would expire. He has fulfilled 99 of the promises and he is able to fulfill the other. Would not I have good reason to trust him that he would fulfill it?
—D. L. Moody

A pattern develops when we pray for a specific request for days and weeks and even years . . .

First pray . . .
    then wait . . .
        then receive.

How we wait upon God's timing says a lot about the depth of our trust in God.

Luis Palau suggests that Saul's "damaging dead end" as king of Israel resulted from his impatient, nervous restlessness . . . his running ahead of God, not waiting for God's signals. Oh, how often do those words classify our own personalities in prayer?

The discipline of daily prayer teaches us to wait or trust in *God's* best. Over the course of our prayer journeys (as we've discussed in previous chapters), we'll discover that much of what we ask God for *is* His will, but the timing is wrong! It is only later, when all the pieces slip neatly into place, that we can ponder and appreciate the extra benefits of what "time and waiting" allowed to transpire.

Accounts in biographies of George Mueller, Hudson Taylor, Jim Elliot, Charles Finney, and Peter and Catherine Marshall detail tremendous stories of waiting and trusting and persevering in prayer, in some cases *for years*, before the answer to a specific prayer request was revealed by God. And so it is in the life of any believer who *prays without giving up*. There is a story of healing, a job opening, a miraculous serendipity in meeting someone special, a financial blessing, or a long-awaited dream fulfilled at last!

Though we may not receive the answer to our prayers as we had envisioned, our responsibility in prayer is to *never* stop waiting, trusting, praying, or expecting of God—the God of Ephesians 3:20, who does immeasurably more than all we could ask or imagine—to answer our request. And what do we find out about God at the end of a long-term wait? O. Hallesby declares, "When He grants our prayers, it is because He loves us. When He does not, it is also because He loves us." We are to trust Him because He loves us.

But be warned! Understanding the dynamics of persevering prayer comes only from the actual *experience* of praying. Phrases, comments, and clichés about prayer sound so inspirational, perhaps even motivational. But only through truly waiting upon God and His response to a prayer request can one develop an inner trust in God that is *sure* of His provision, though the details are unseen.

Patience and perseverance in prayer come not from begging God, but from waiting on Him. The discipline of waiting includes asking God if we are praying rightly, if we've heard His promise accurately. It involves evaluating our motives, honestly examining if they are impure or selfish, and being able to acknowl-

150

edge when our hopes are centered on something other than God's will.

Perseverance in prayer includes a willingness to let Him alter or change our requests in prayer according to His plan. And especially over an extended time of seeming silence, we who wait on God must be careful that our persistence in prayer does not become anxiety that saps strength; rather, it should be anticipation of His will that increases the endurance to persevere. Again, O. Hallesby captures the timing of prayer: "The more completely you cease being concerned about the TIME in which your prayers are to be answered, the more freedom you'll enjoy in your prayer life!"

CHAPTER

15

Prayer Reveals God's Plan and Our Purpose

James 1:5 says, "If any of you lacks wisdom, he should ask God, who gives generously to all without finding fault, and it will be given to him." I believe that God's Word means what it says. If God says it is okay to ask Him for wisdom to make decisions or plans, it would demean this Scripture if I wondered and worried about whether God *wanted* to show me His will. I'd emotionally be a mess, "driven and tossed by the wind," as James continues to warn the person who doubts once God has shown him His answers. The Word gives one the complete confidence that if and when one asks, God will answer!

First John 5:14–15 reiterates that verse by stating, "This is the confidence we have in approaching God: that if we ask anything according to his will, he hears us. And if we know that he hears us—whatever we ask—we know that we have what we asked of him."

Sometimes God's Word is so loud and clear that we're afraid or intimidated by its directives, especially when it comes to asking, hearing, knowing, and doing His will. We get tripped up by the timing of the answer or by people around us who may negatively influence us or by a fear of looking foolish. That's when looking at the Word for real-life illustrations of those who sought God's specific plan—and received it—provides encouragement to believe that the principle is the same for *anyone* who loves God and fears Him.

What would Israel have been like without the prayers and obedience of Joseph, Moses, Daniel, and Samuel asking and receiving God's specific direction for travel, battle, rations, words of knowledge, and strength? And why would we in our life's journey of battles, travels, and physical needs be any less needy of God's specific direction?

Granted, there are a few "minor" prerequisites for knowing God's will, as the psalmist mentions in Psalm 25:12, "Who, then, is the man that fears the LORD? He will instruct him in the way chosen for him." And he continues, "The LORD confides in those who fear him; he makes his covenant known to them" (v. 14).

I am convinced by Scripture and personal experience that "fearing" God—loving, revering, and obeying Him—is the pathway to asking for and obtaining God's will for one's life. From one's personal relationship with God, one gains the assurance that He indeed *has* a specific plan for one's life. Then as Matthew 21:22 says, "If you believe [in what He has shown you is the *way* to pray . . . His will], you will receive whatever you ask for in prayer."

In the large and small circumstances, in the lives of the weak and strong, for the famous and infamous, God has a plan. Psalm 139:16 points to that truth:

> All the days ordained for me
> were written in your book
> before one of them came to be.

May I be so bold to say that *when* I have asked, I have always received my "marching orders," and because God has shown me the way, I know where I am going. I have received a call, and I'm following.

153

Ask for His will,
> *believe* in what God says is yours, until you
> > *receive all* that He has for you.

In the book *Guide to Prayer for Ministers and Other Servants* is an excerpt from *The Art of Prayer,* which offers a beautiful description of asking, receiving, and even writing down prayers:

> You write that at times, during prayer, a solution to some problem that perplexes you in your spiritual life comes out of itself from an unknown source. This is good. It is the true Christian way of being taught God's truth. Here the promise is fulfilled and they shall be taught of God (John 6:45). So indeed it is. Truths are inscribed in the heart by the finger of God and remain there firm and indelible. Do not neglect these truths which God inscribes but write them down. And upon writing down the direction one believes God is taking them and acting upon what is written down I have no doubt or reservation to say one will know God's will for their lives.

The book of Proverbs is full of sage advice, not the least of which is this: "In all your ways, acknowledge Him, and He shall direct your paths" (3:6, NKJV). Which of us would not want to have the directions to the very best of all possible plans made available? A habit of inquiring of God in all situations will inevitably—as promised—reveal His plans.

CHAPTER

16

Prayer Releases God's Power

Prayer releases God's power
. . . in the life of a person.
. . . in the life of a church.
. . . in the life of a community.
. . . in the life of a country.

Has not prayer been the means used to escort a sinner through the gates of salvation into eternal life? Has not prayer been the vehicle that ushers in the Holy Spirit's power to bring about physical healing and to turn one man—even a convict—from the depths of sin and ungodliness (whether it be the apostle Paul or a David Wilkerson) into an itinerant evangelist? Does not prayer precede miracles of inner healing? Is not concerted prayer the groundwork for revival?

In the New International Version of the Bible, James 5:16 reads, "The prayer of a righteous man is powerful and effective," and in the New King James Version it is stated, "The effective, fervent prayer of a righteous man avails much." If prayer had no power or even little power, what would be its purpose? Since prayer is presented as an effective *source of power* for the believer, it appears unwise, even foolish, to approach life without it—at least as foolish as it would be to go into enemy territory without weapons for defense.

Could it be that we neglect prayer because we don't have a need for power in our daily lives? I doubt that. I know not *one* life that has no struggle or disappointment, does not face some opposition or illness, has not experienced pain or tragedy to some degree, and therefore has no *need* for God's power to be released.

So, to whom is the power available, and how does prayer release God's power? Forgive me if my answer seems simple, but I am convinced the source of God's power to change, rearrange, create, move, and transform a believer's life is the person of the Holy Spirit.

I say this not because I am an expert on the subject, but because I have experienced and witnessed supernatural power and intervention in countless circumstances where, through an invitation to the Holy Spirit in prayer, God's power was released to avail much! Through reading books such as *The Helper* by Catherine Marshall and having been led to Christ by an enthusiastic, charismatic Christian, I have been open to and intrigued by the Holy Spirit of God. All the while, though, I've observed many people who are intimidated by the same powerful Holy Spirit, avoiding and essentially ignoring Him and His available power.

For whatever reason—misunderstanding, fear, or doubt—when the Holy Spirit is not invited by believers into their lives or circumstances, it appears they have pulled the plug to their power source—God Himself.

Not only is the book of Acts an incredible account of the works and power of the Holy Spirit, but Jesus Himself implored His disciples to wait upon and cling to His Holy Spirit. Jesus promised that His Spirit would *empower* them (Acts 1:8) and teach them truth and provide counsel. He would take what was His and make it *known* to them (John 15—16)! Paul prayed for the Ephesians: "I pray that out of his [God's] glorious riches he may strengthen you with power through his

Spirit in your inner being, so that Christ may dwell in your hearts through faith" (Eph. 3:16–17).

I am not naive enough to assume that my few words of testimony and Scripture regarding the power released when one invites the person of the Holy Spirit into one's life or circumstances will dramatically convince or change one's thoughts or beliefs in this area. But I am willing to challenge anyone who will be open to leaving the supernatural releasing of power up to God! To do this, pray daily (at the start of each new day and after a regular time of confession) this simple prayer:

> *Lord, fill me up to **overflowing** with Your Holy Spirit this day. I commit my ways to You.*

Then wait in anticipation for God's power to be released within your life in (perhaps) both unusual and supernatural ways.

Jesus said, "If you then, though you are evil, know how to give good gifts to your children, how much more will your Father in heaven give the Holy Spirit to those who ask him!" (Luke 11:13).

Prayer Unleashes
Love for God

Andrew Murray asked, "What is it that makes the inner chamber so powerless?" And he answered his own question by saying, "The world's fellowship is more attractive than being alone with the Heavenly Father."

All the words and sentences in this book have urged each of us to look at our relationship with God through prayer.

Is prayer the intimate time with God that is increasing as we pass through daily experiences?

Is prayer the confidential conversations we have with our Best Friend?

Is prayer an expression of our commitment to God?

For some of us, if it is, we're in trouble.

Should our love relationship with God be considered any differently from our other relationships? If we, for whatever reason, neglect to spend time with Him, is that love? I have found no better challenge that I could leave you with than this from *The God Who Comes* by Carlo Carretto:

If a fiance telephones his fiancee to tell her, "I'm sorry, this evening I can't come, I've so much work!", there is nothing wrong. But if it is the thousandth time he has made the same call, he has not been to see her in weeks on the excuse of work outings with friends, it is more serious—rather, it is quite clear: this is not love. . . .

If you don't pray, if you are not searching for a personal relationship with God, if you don't stay with him for long periods in order to know him, study him, understand him, little by little you will start forgetting him, your memory will weaken, you will no longer recognize him. You will not be able to, because you will no longer know how to love.

. . . Have you
been not praying,
not seeking him personally
because you don't love him or
because you have no time?

My purpose in writing this book is to motivate and inspire every reader to plan on and look forward to spending time with God. In the prayer workshops and seminars that I conduct, I would feel negligent if I just "told a good story," but did not challenge the people to evaluate their present prayer lives and *then* make a practical decision in relationship to spending time with the Lord. Therefore, if you've not already made prayer a daily part of your life, and you feel compelled by God's Holy Spirit to make such a commitment of your time and love, I would ask you to join me in the following prayer:

O Lord, I believe that You have a personal plan for my life that will affect the world around me for You if I will daily spend time with You in prayer and diligently look for You and listen to You through Your Word and Spirit. Cause me to meet with You every day in a regular appointment for the rest of my life. Fill me with Your Holy Spirit, woo me to Your Word, increase my faith, and develop within me an incredible love for You. I ask these things in Jesus' name. Amen.

159

About the Author

Becky Tirabassi is founder of My Partner Ministries, an inspirational and motivational speaking and writing ministry to all age groups.

She appears regularly on local and national media—both television and radio—including "Focus on the Family" and "Chapel of the Air." Tirabassi was a guest speaker at the Northeastern Ohio Billy Graham Crusade on June 9, 1994. Articles about and by Becky can be found in *Aspire* and *Today's Christian Woman* magazines.

She lives in Newport Beach, California, with her husband, Roger, and sixteen-year-old son, Jake.

If you are interested in booking a motivational prayer workshop or in some other aspect of Becky Tirabassi's ministry, please write or call

My Partner Ministries
P.O. Box 9672
Newport Beach, CA 92660

1-800-444-6189